THE HOMESTEADER'S KITCHEN

THE
HOMESTEADER'S
KITCHEN

RECIPES FROM FARM TO TABLE

ROBIN BURNSIDE

GIBBS SMITH
TO ENRICH AND INSPIRE HUMANKIND

First Edition
14 13 12 11 10   5 4 3 2 1

Text © 2010 Robin Burnside
Photographs © 2010 Kodiak Greenwood

Published by
Gibbs Smith
P.O. Box 667
Layton, Utah 84041

1.800.835.4993 orders
www.gibbs-smith.com

Designed by Blue Design (www.bluedes.com)
Printed and bound in Hong Kong
Gibbs Smith books are printed on paper produced
from sustainable PEFC-certified forest/controlled
wood source.
Learn more at: www.pefc.org

Library of Congress Cataloging-in-Publication Data

Burnside, Robin.
  The homesteader's kitchen : recipes from farm to
table / Robin Burnside. — 1st ed.
      p. cm.
  Includes index.
  ISBN-13: 978-1-4236-0058-9
  ISBN-10: 1-4236-0058-4
  1. Cookery (Natural foods) I. Title.
  TX741.B86 2010
  641.5'636—dc22
                              2010006852

With deep gratitude, this book is dedicated to
my husband Bill for his unconditional love and
endless support; to my children Joshua, Crystal,
Nathaniel, and Theron for their exceptional
palates, feedback, and helping hands; and to all
my precious grandchildren for their boundless
enthusiasm and love of fresh whole foods.

C O N T E N T S

Acknowledgments 8

Introduction 11

    How to Get Started 13

    Basic Kitchen Equipment 14

    Stocking the Larder 17

Beverages 19

Morning Meals 31

Soups, Sauces, and Gravies 49

Salads and Salad Dressings 65

Vegetarian Entrées 97

Fish, Poultry, and Meat Entrées 115

Embellishments 129

Breads 153

Desserts 167

Glossary 185

Index 188

Acknowledgments

My sincere appreciation and thanks to all the family, friends, and colleagues who have shared this rich, varied, and nourishing path with me. It has truly been my pleasure.

This book had its roots in my childhood and I am eternally grateful to both of my grandmothers. From Grandma Oddo, my sweet old-fashioned granny, I learned to serve the family; my Bohemian Grandma Jane taught me the business side of preparing and serving beautiful food in a commercial setting. They are at the core of my passion for fresh whole foods, lovingly prepared. Their spirits are alive in these pages and in my heart as well.

To all of the restaurant owners, cooks, waitresses, waiters, dishwashers, purveyors, and delivery folks who have worked, played, and "jammed or improvised" along with me in many a commercial kitchen, I am truly thankful to have shared in the experience of co-creating wholesome food, growing ourselves, and feeding the world! As professionals, when asked, they have also volunteered their skills, time, and energy for good causes, event after event, festival after festival, year after year and I am deeply grateful.

My appreciation goes out to Jane Militich, Bob Wilson, Richard Ware, Charlie Cascio, John Blunt, Marla Bell, Narayana, Jack-of-all-trades, Lolly Fassett, Holly Fassett, Barbara Woyt, Grace and Bob Swanson, Amigo Bob, Michele Guthrie, Bunny Gries, Katee Armstrong, Rachel Fann, Rollie Ogden, Jennifer Dean, Bill Herr, Allan Mello, Hidden Mountain, Andrea Ahlgren-Shirley, Robin Ahlgren, Liam McDermott, Chloe Conger, and Shani Cranston—I have learned something special from each of you.

Being in the kitchen with friends and family is one of my favorite things—and there is no place like home. Many of my loved ones are excellent cooks who have freely shared their wisdom and experience, inspiring me to stretch myself in new ways. A heartfelt thanks to Rosemary Fosse, Sylvia Burnside, Joshua Wilson, Crystal Gries, Tafay Lindeman, Alia Pratt, Peggy and Dick Horan, Eric and Ruth Jensen, Copperwoman, Martine Algiers, Ginna Bell-Bragg, Alicia Bay Laurel, Sarah Bly, Kate Healey, Lygia Chappellet, Torre Forrest, Jeannie Ford, Emily Mann, Wing Hodas, and Lizzy Bechtold. Being in the kitchen with each of you has truly been a blessing. I look forward to the many gatherings, holidays, and celebrations to come.

Growing food, especially for a large family, takes a lot of work, skill, water, and patience. To supplement the offerings from my own garden, I rely on local farmers markets. Purchasing something fresh and flavorful from each of my favorite vendors is an outing I always look forward to. To Steve, Syndey, Michael, Gary, Jack, Maria and Osias, Loretta, Cristina, Ester, Tom, Dave, Pearl, Jay, Ross, Claudia, Logan, Diego, Shirley, Ben, and all the other wonderful organic farmers on the central California coast and in Baja California Sur, my deepest thanks—keep on growing!

I would like to give special appreciation to Nani Steele for all her encouragement, constructive feedback, and fabulous food styling. From the beginning of this project, her loving kindness and expertise has helped me transform the challenging process of writing a book into a wonderful new journey. Keep on dreaming, writing, and inspiring others with your bright light and sweet smile.

The photos Kodiak Greenwood took for this book are simply amazing. I have known him since birth, and it has been an honor to watch him grow and develop this special talent. Together we went to several farmers markets and numerous neighborhood gardens as well as home and commercial kitchens to set up the shots. He skillfully transformed beautiful images into art, and the manuscript came to life. I am grateful to have these extraordinary photographs woven throughout this book.

I would like to thank Gibbs Smith, Hollie Keith, Michelle Branson, and all the folks at Gibbs Smith for their trust, support, and patience. Without your interest and generosity, this book would have never been written. I have learned much throughout the process, while growing in unimaginable ways, and I am truly grateful.

To my parents, Rosemary Fosse and Bob Burnside, your understanding, support, and faith has given me the courage to spread my wings and embrace this wonderful life I've been given, thanks again.

And to my family, Bill, Josh, Crystal, Nathaniel, Theron, Tafay, Tom, Ivan, Athena, Ethan, Tanith, Weston, and Rayden, words can not convey my gratitude for your caring and support while I worked my way through visioning, writing, recipe testing, and editing this project. I give thanks for the life we share and the love that grows in my heart for you all each and every day.

Introduction

Traditionally, the kitchen is the heart and hearth of the home—the place where family and friends gather for connection and nourishment. We are drawn to the warmth of the oven fires, the flavors ripening in the air, and the promise of the meal to come. The recipes in this book are dedicated to these simple pleasures that build relationships and community, warm our hearts, nourish our bodies, and feed our souls.

In an era that values the convenience of processed and fast food, basic cooking knowledge is becoming a lost art. The very act of making a meal from scratch fills an ancient need in us that cannot be met with even the tastiest store-bought products. We miss that primal process of making food; the creativity and attention it demands, the delightful alchemy of ingredients coming together to form so much more than the sum of their parts, and the personal connection we feel to the meal. For some, cooking from scratch can be intimidating, but preparing wholesome meals can be as easy or as complicated as you want to make it. Often, less is more. Simple preparations retain the distinct, fresh flavors of whole foods, and, with careful planning, a well-stocked larder, and a good supply of fresh organic produce, it takes just a few moments from a busy life.

With basic kitchen skills, creative recipes, and tricks-of-the-trade, you can easily transform a humble dish into a culinary masterpiece. A little savory sauce, dollop of pesto, or freshly chopped herbs can brighten the simplest meal, and add a special personal touch. *The Homesteader's Kitchen* has easy-to-follow recipes that will inspire even the novice cook to don an apron and enjoy time in the kitchen making wholesome meals, tasty embellishments, and luscious desserts for everyday fare as well as special celebrations.

I had my first experiences working in a kitchen while visiting my Italian-born grandmother as a young girl. Seeing that I couldn't wait to get my hands in the dough, my grandfather made me a little stool so I could work at my grandmother's side. From sink to stove, I moved the stool back and forth, scraping it across worn wooden floors, trying to keep up with each magical moment.

Grocery shopping with Grandma Oddo was always an adventure. She knew that flavorful meals began with good-quality ingredients, and we would go from store to store to find just what she needed. I can still remember her directing the butcher on how to cut her meat just so; encouraging the deli owner to stock big blocks of fresh ricotta cheese, semolina pasta, and fruity olive oil; and pleading with the produce man to carry fresh fava beans and other interesting vegetables so she could give us a taste of "the old country."

My paternal grandmother was a restaurant owner and caterer—a trusted professional in our community known for her ability to make everyone feel comfortable and cared for. Grandma Jane introduced me to the art of feeding a crowd. I remember standing proudly at her side on the serving line as she greeted her guests. Family and business were well entwined and, in my teens, I became her strong-backed, inquisitive, and attentive apprentice.

Cooking with my grandmothers inspired the foundation of my own professional and family life—memorable meals made with fresh high-quality ingredients that are prepared simply, with care and imagination, by loving hands.

As a college student, I supported myself working in restaurants, and studied with many talented chefs, managers, and owners who valued my experience and were willing to apprentice me in the trade. I saw that treating the staff with kindness, and, of course, serving great food was the best formula for success in the challenging restaurant business.

My first solo venture was making wholesale specialty cheesecakes for Monterey area restaurants out of a home kitchen. As the business grew, we moved to a commercial facility—a former little donut shop with a big kitchen in the heart of town. After extensive remodeling we opened the Carmel Café and began serving breakfast, lunch, and dinner. In the back room we made cheesecakes for our wholesale accounts and began catering private parties and weddings for friends and neighbors. Our little family-run restaurant was known around town for having a delicious and diverse menu that could please a wide variety of palates with nourishing food for the whole family.

After several prosperous years we sold the Carmel Café, moved to Big Sur, and opened Café Amphora at Nepenthe. It had a small but very efficient kitchen, and the front serving area looked out onto a large open deck where customers could watch soaring hawks, spouting whales, and fabulous sunsets as they enjoyed their meals. We served breakfast and lunch throughout the day and also hosted special events and weddings on warm summer evenings.

After Café Amphora, I worked as a private chef and caterer. I also managed the kitchen at the Esalen Institute for five years, with its abundant gorgeous garden, feeding 250 to 300 people three wholesome meals a day in a dynamic community setting.

My favorite time in the kitchen, however, is spent preparing celebration meals at home with family and friends. Everyone contributes something special to the occasion.

We come together in the kitchen, infusing prana (life-energy) into the food with our laughter and love. Cooking together strengthens relationships more than any other activity we can do as a family, and teaches children important life skills. This book is the fruit of my personal and professional journey preparing nutritious and delicious food for myself, my family, and my community—a passion that began in my teens and evolved into a forty-year culinary career. In these pages you will find inspirational recipes, money-saving tips on shopping, helpful ideas for entertaining, and beautiful images to inspire your own creativity—enjoy the experience!

HOW TO GET STARTED

Begin creating your kitchen by doing what you can, wherever you are, with what you have on hand. Your kitchen can be a knife and cutting board balanced on the tailgate of your truck parked at the beach, or wherever you are. Good light, a clean workspace, and willing hands are all that is needed to begin. Whether you live in a studio apartment with a toaster oven, or a big house with a designer kitchen, you can bring the farm to the table. For me, the serving environment is a key component of the experience. Begin by setting out a basket of ripening fruit, a pretty potted plant, or some freshly cut flowers or herbs.

Bringing the beauty of the outdoors into your kitchen will enhance your experience and entice your loved ones to join you.

Imagine knowing where your food comes from, saving money and the environment, all while supporting your local economy. Yes, it takes a commitment, and the rewards are well worth the effort. You can make a significant difference by using cloth shopping bags, purchasing staples in bulk, and buying organic produce from local farmers. If you commit to buying local produce, you will benefit from fresher, more vital, and nutrient-rich food. By eating seasonally, your body will be more in harmony with natural cycles, getting grounding root veggies in fall and winter, cleansing young greens in the spring, fruits in the summer, and so on. Shop at farmers markets and develop relationships with the people who grow your food. One of the most fun, easy, and economical ways to get your fruits and veggies is to join a community supported agriculture group (CSA) and receive a box of their weekly harvest throughout the growing season. To further economize, look for the best price on whole food staples, which can vary considerably from store to store. Join a co-operative buying group, or gather friends and neighbors and start your own co-op or buyers club.

Foraging for wild foods and growing your own garden is time well spent, and can lower your food bill considerably. Even if you don't have space for a garden, planting herbs, tomatoes, and greens in a few pots or barrels will keep you connected to the natural world, while providing fresh accents to complement your meals. A snippet of thyme or parsley, a few vine-ripened tomatoes, or a handful of fresh-picked greens can make an ordinary meal spectacular. These simple changes will reduce packaging and distribution costs, lower your overall food bill, and improve the quality of the ingredients you use.

In my kitchen, I choose organic whole foods, produce, and dairy products. I purchase only organic, hormone-free, and preferably grass-fed meats and free-range poultry whenever possible. The term organic is used for products that have not been treated with herbicides, pesticides, or industrial fertilizers. They generally do not include irradiated food, genetically modified crops, artificial flavorings, preservatives, or colorings. Preparing meals from real, whole foods is easier than you think, and the rewards are many for you, your loved ones, and the planet. We can have a profound impact on the earth and our health with our food choices, and every little bit counts.

BASIC KITCHEN EQUIPMENT

Good-quality equipment will add to your enjoyment and success in the kitchen. Stainless-steel pots and pans, cast-iron skillets, and enamel or glass are my tools of choice. While aluminum is lightweight and inexpensive, it reacts with acid foods and salt, leaching metal into food and compromising our health. I have never felt comfortable cooking on a plastic surface, even if it is specially made for high heat, and do not use nonstick pans or other new-age materials. My nonstick pan is a well-seasoned cast-iron skillet and it works just fine. The basics also include: a big, heavy-bottom stainless-steel soup pot; several sizes of stainless-steel or flame-proof glass saucepans with lids; a stainless-steel steamer fan; a 10 to 12-inch cast-iron skillet, and an ovenproof glass or enamel baking dish. You may also consider adding these non-essential but useful items to your kitchen: an Oriental steel wok, an enamel-covered iron pot, a clay cooker, and an outdoor smoker or barbecue.

Cake pans and muffin tins are the only aluminum equipment I use in my kitchen, and I always line them with baking paper before pouring in the batter. Your baking equipment should include a couple of glass or ceramic bread pans, a large ovenproof rectangular glass baking dish, and a smaller square one, a flat baking sheet, a fluted-edge tart pan with removable rim, a couple of 10-inch glass pie plates, and two 9-inch cake pans.

Professional quality knives are essential tools to invest in and, when properly cared for, will serve you well. Keeping knives sharp is a must. A dull knife can be dangerous, especially when the blade is thin and wiggles as you cut. The best quality metal knives will have a heavy blade extending up through the middle of the handle, preferably made of hard wood, and secured with sturdy rivets. It is also a good idea to invest in a sharpening stone, and use it often, for safety, ease, and enjoyment. Carbon steel sharpens easily, but tends to stain with certain foods and needs to be regularly sharpened. A stainless-steel blade is more difficult to hone, but will stay sharp longer. I love ceramic knives as they hold their edge longer than steel, are very lightweight, and are perfectly balanced. A well-cared-for ceramic blade does not need sharpening, will give you years of service, and makes cutting and chopping a pleasure. My favorite all-purpose knife is a 7-inch rectangular Oriental style with a wooden handle that feels stable and works well for most of what I do. I also use a 10-inch chef's knife for bigger jobs and one with a thinner blade for carving. An 8-inch serrated bread knife is great for slicing tomatoes as well as bread. I use a small paring knife for peeling apples and other small jobs. When purchasing knives, be sure to choose a variety of sizes and shapes, and before you buy a knife, test it for comfort and balance in your hand.

I like to work with a good-size cutting board that can comfortably fit all of my ingredients. There are many choices when it comes to cutting boards. I prefer to use natural materials because the plastic boards tend to absorb odors and colors, and their surface often gets nicked and rough. Solid hardwood cutting boards are lovely, but they can be very expensive. For the best value, I recommend a big, professional-quality hardwood or renewable bamboo laminated (butcher block) cutting board and a couple of smaller boards around for little jobs and helpful friends. Before using a new solid or laminated-wood board, season it with a little oil—mineral, coconut, walnut, or almond—to seal it, and prevent staining and the absorption of food odors and bacteria. I like to complete the process with a light coat of beeswax, which fills in the cracks and leaves a beautiful shine when buffed with a cloth. When you've finished using your board, be sure to wash it with hot soapy water and rinse well. It is important that you wet both sides of your wood cutting board each time you wash it, being sure to dry it completely on both sides to prevent warping and cracking. To remove stubborn odors and freshen your cutting board, rub the surface with the cut half of a lemon and wash as usual. A good-quality cutting board will last for generations if it is properly cared for.

Stainless-steel, glass, and ceramic mixing bowls are preferable to plastic ones, which can stain, hold flavors, and leech plastic into warm food. Have one or two large mixing bowls and a variety of smaller ones at hand. Wooden bowls are lightweight, attractive and sturdy vessels for serving salads, crackers, dips, nuts, or other treats.

Plastic containers are convenient for storing foods and can be recycled from products you purchase; however, glass mason jars are my favorite storage containers. With an assortment of wide-mouthed pint, quart, half-gallon, and gallon jars, I can store almost anything, including dried goods, liquids, and leftovers—hot or cold. The foods are easy to see, well-sealed for freshness, and the jars can be thoroughly cleaned. Using glass containers has the added bonus of significantly reducing my consumption of plastics.

Fancy kitchen utensils are enticing and often expensive. So, begin with these basics: a set of measuring cups and spoons; flexible rubber spatulas; a soup ladle; a metal spatula; several long-handled stainless-steel and wooden spoons; one large and one small stainless-steel whisk; long-handled stainless-steel tongs; a potato masher; heavy kitchen scissors; a heavy-duty can opener; a small glass or stainless-steel citrus juicer; a stainless-steel multi-sided grater; a large and a small wire-mesh strainer; and a big, stainless-steel colander. Other useful tools include a stainless-steel teakettle, a salad spinner, and a pepper grinder. One of my favorite tools is a stainless-steel rasp, or fine grater. I use it almost every day to grate fresh gingerroot and nutmeg. It also removes the zest from citrus better than any other tool I have found. A mandolin quickly and uniformly slices foods and is a great addition to any kitchen. You will also need a stack of absorbent cotton or linen kitchen towels, several thick pot holders, and a few pretty serving platters in various sizes.

I must admit that I am deeply attached to my machines and use them daily in preparing many different dishes. Whole foods can be made into wonderful sauces, dressings, and many a fine meal quickly and easily with a small coffee grinder, vegetable juicer, blender, food processor, and dehydrator—all invaluable tools in my kitchen. If you prefer to avoid machines or just don't have them in your kitchen, a knife and cutting board, hand grinder, wire whisk, or traditional mortar and pestle will work for the recipes that do not explicitly call for a blender.

Quality kitchen equipment can be found in specialty stores, online, and from restaurant suppliers. I have found some of my best tools at rummage sales, secondhand stores, and used restaurant equipment outlets at a fraction of the cost of purchasing them new. Well-made equipment and tools last longer, work better, and bring greater pleasure to the process. In the end they are more economical than cheaper versions and can last for generations. I encourage you to make the investment, because having the right tools is always more efficient and fun.

STOCKING THE LARDER

A well-stocked larder and refrigerator, along with an abundance of fresh produce from your garden or a local farmers market, will inspire creativity and improve the flavor and quality of your meals. This is a list of the basic ingredients for a whole foods larder. Choose and stock what you like to eat, and ingredients for your most common meals. Whenever possible, purchase staples—like grains, nuts, seeds, and legumes—in bulk and save the extra cost of packaging. Shop at a local farmers market, co-op, natural food store, supermarket, or neighborhood grocery store and purchase organically grown products whenever possible. You will be rewarded with flavorful and nutritious meals while doing your part to create a sustainable future for us all. For more information on unfamiliar ingredients, please refer to the glossary (page 185).

BEANS AND LEGUMES

- Beans (dried or canned)
- Black (turtle)
- Cannellini (white kidney)
- Garbanzo (chickpeas)
- Kidney (red)
- Lentils (brown and small green)
- Limas (butter beans)
- Peas (split green, red, and yellow)
- Pinto (pink)
- White (great Northern or navy)

DRIED FRUIT, PREFERABLY UNSULFURED

- Apples
- Apricots
- Cherries (pitted)
- Coconut (dried and shredded)
- Currants
- Dates
- Figs
- Nectarines
- Peaches
- Pears
- Prunes
- Raisins

DRIED HERBS AND SPICES

- Basil
- Bay leaf
- Cardamom
- Cayenne
- Chili powder
- Cinnamon (powder and whole sticks)
- Cloves (powder and whole)
- Coriander
- Cumin
- Curry powder
- Dill
- Ginger powder
- Italian seasoning (a blend of dried basil, marjoram, oregano, rosemary and thyme leaves
- Mustard (powder and whole seeds)
- Nutmeg (ground and whole)
- Oregano
- Paprika
- Pepper (black or white, ground and whole peppercorns)
- Red pepper (crushed)
- Rosemary
- Sage
- Tarragon
- Thyme
- Turmeric

FLOURS

- Corn flour or masa harina
- Cornmeal
- Rye flour
- Spelt flour
- Unbleached white flour
- Whole wheat bread flour
- Whole wheat pastry flour

FRESH VEGETABLES

- Carrots
- Celery
- Garlic
- Gingerroot
- Greens (cabbage, chard, cilantro, kale, lettuce, parsley, or other leafy seasonal greens)
- Onions (Spanish yellow, red, sweet white, shallots, leeks, scallions, including seasonal and local varieties)
- Potatoes (red, russets, yams, and heirloom varieties)
- Summer squash (patty-pan, yellow crookneck, zucchini, and heirloom varieties)
- Winter squash (acorn, butternut, delicata, turban, or other heirloom varieties)

FRESH FRUIT

- Apples
- Avocados
- Bananas
- Berries* (blackberries, blueberries, raspberries, and strawberries)
- Figs*
- Grapes*
- Grapefruit
- Lemons
- Limes
- Melons* (cantaloupe, casaba, honeydew, watermelon, and other heirloom varieties)
- Oranges
- Pears*
- Pit fruit* (apricots, cherries, nectarines, peaches, and plums)
- Tangerines*
- Tomatoes* (seasonal locally-grown varieties have the best flavor)

Notes short seasonal availability

LEAVENINGS AND FLAVORINGS

- Baking powder
- Baking soda
- Baking yeast
- Sea salt
- Almond extract
- Vanilla extract

NUTS AND SEEDS

- Almonds
- Cashews
- Flax seeds
- Hazelnuts
- Peanuts
- Pecans
- Popcorn
- Pumpkin seeds
- Sesame seeds (brown and black)
- Sprouting seeds (see page 67)
- Sunflower seeds
- Walnuts

OILS

- Coconut
- Extra virgin olive
- Flax seed
- Rice bran
- Sesame (unrefined and toasted)
- Optional: corn, sunflower, safflower, peanut, and canola

PREPARED AND CONVENIENCE FOODS

- Almond butter
- Coconut milk (canned)
- Corn chips
- Non-fat dry milk powder
- Olives
- Peanut butter
- Rice or soy milk
- Sauerkraut and pickles
- Tahini (raw or toasted)
- Veggie burgers
- Whole or sprouted grain bread

REFRIGERATED AND FROZEN GOODS

- Cheese (a variety of your favorites)
- Eggs
- Mayonnaise (prepared or homemade)
- Milk
- Tempeh
- Tofu
- Tortillas (corn and sprouted wheat)
- Unsalted butter
- Vegenaise
- Yogurt

GRAINS AND PASTAS

- Barley
- Brown rice, short or long grain
- Millet
- Oats, rolled and whole groats
- Quinoa
- Rice and Whole Grain Pasta
- Wild rice

SEASONINGS AND CONDIMENTS

- Bottled hot sauce (Thai and Mexican style)
- Dried mushrooms
- Ketchup
- Mustard (stone-ground and Dijon)
- Nutritional yeast (large flakes taste best)
- Sea vegetables (powdered dulse, kombu, and other kelp)
- Tamari, shoyu, or soy sauce
- Vegetable broth powder
- Vinegar (apple cider, balsamic, rice wine, and special brews of choice)

SWEETENERS

- Agave nectar
- Maple syrup
- Molasses
- Raw honey
- Sucanat or Rapadura

Fresh Fruit Smoothies

Smoothies for breakfast made with fresh fruit, fruit juice, dairy or grain milk, yogurt, seeds, and nuts will fuel you well into the day with wholesome goodness. Adding your favorite green super food or other supplements to the mix makes a smoothie into a quick and complete high-protein meal, a blessing when you are short on time. Peeling and freezing ripe bananas works well for chilling these creamy drinks, and you can also add a little ice if you like a frosty texture. Frozen fruit, especially the tropical varieties, works well in smoothies, but locally grown fresh fruit is always my first choice. Experiment with your favorite seasonal offerings as they appear throughout the year and enjoy enzyme rich, flavorful, and nutritious smoothies. Here are a few combinations to help inspire you to make smoothies a regular part of your diet.

Creamy Mango-Coconut

MAKES 1 LARGE SERVING

¹/₄ cup cashews, soaked in
1 cup of water for 4 to 6
hours or overnight

1 fresh mango, peeled, seeded,
and chopped, or 1 cup
frozen mango pieces

1 frozen banana

¹/₂ cup plain Yogurt (page 141)

1 whole fresh young coconut,
water and cream scraped
from the inside of the shell*

1 tablespoon agave nectar

Strain and rinse the cashews. Place all of the ingredients into a blender and purée on high until smooth and creamy. If the smoothie is too thick for your liking, just add a little milk or fruit juice to the mixture. Pour into a large glass and enjoy.

* A combination of 1 cup organic canned coconut water and ¹/₂ cup organic canned whole coconut milk can be substituted in a pinch. However, canned coconut does not have the live enzymes that are found in whole fresh coconuts.

Kiwi Berry

MAKES 1 LARGE SERVING

2 kiwi, peeled and sliced

1 frozen banana

¹/₂ cup fresh blueberries

1 cup whole fresh strawberries

1¹/₂ cups freshly squeezed
orange juice

1 tablespoon honey, optional

Place all of the ingredients into a blender and purée on high until smooth and creamy. If the smoothie is too thick for your liking, just add a little more juice to the mixture. Pour into a large glass and enjoy.

Opening a fresh young coconut is easier than you think. You will need a big heavy knife or cleaver. Hold the coconut firmly and stabilize on the table before you begin. With small strokes, carefully cut the white covering off the top, or pointed end, to expose the hard shell. Look for a little brown circular ridge and wiggle the tip of the knife just under it and press it into the shell. Give a whack to the end of the knife handle to secure it in place. Lodge the blade into the shell by lifting the coconut with your other hand while striking the knife and coconut down onto a sturdy table or counter in one continuous motion. Once the top has split open, quickly put the coconut upright to save the juice. With the tip of the knife pressed firmly into the shell, slowly push the knife away from you while carefully turning the coconut in a circle around the top until it pops off. Pour the water into a glass, and with a large spoon, scrape the custard-like meat from the inside of the shell. You only want the white layer, not bits of shell, so be careful not to press too hard as you go. This delicacy is definitely worth all the work and is a valuable food source that nourishes our body on a core level.

Cherry, Peach, and Hemp Seed

MAKES 1 LARGE SERVING

....

$1/2$ cup fresh cherries, pitted

1 large fresh peach, cut into chunks

$1/4$ cup hulled hemp seeds

1 cup whole milk or almond
   milk (see Hazelnut Hemp
   Mylk, page 28)

1 tablespoon honey

Place all of the ingredients into a blender and purée on high until smooth and creamy. If the smoothie is too thick for your liking, just add a little more milk to the mixture. Pour into a large glass and enjoy.

Tropical Delight

MAKES 1 LARGE SERVING

....

1 whole fresh young coconut,
   water and cream scraped
   from the inside of the shell*

1 frozen banana

$1/4$ of a fresh medium-size papaya,
   peeled and cut into chunks

$1/2$ cup chunks fresh pineapple

1 cup pineapple juice (more
   or less, depending on
   volume of coconut milk)

1 tablespoon agave nectar, optional

1 teaspoon maca powder

Place all of the ingredients into a blender and purée on high until smooth and creamy. If the smoothie is too thick for your liking, just add a little more juice or milk to the mixture. Pour into a large glass and enjoy.

*A combination of 1 cup organic canned coconut water and $1/2$ cup organic canned whole coconut milk can be substituted. However, canned coconut does not have the live enzymes that are found in whole fresh coconuts.

Pear and Feijoa

....

1/4 cup sunflower seeds, soaked overnight in one cup of water

1 large pear

3 medium-size feijoas, peeled and sliced (see glossary)

1 cup whole milk or grain milk (see Hazelnut Hemp Mylk, page 28)

1/2 cup ice or a frozen banana

1 tablespoon agave nectar, optional

Strain and rinse the sunflower seeds. Place all of the ingredients into a blender and purée on high until smooth and creamy. If the smoothie is too thick for your liking, just add a little more milk to the mixture. Pour into a large glass and enjoy.

Dreamy Cashew Date

....

1/2 cup cashews, soaked overnight in 2 cups of water

1/2 cup dates, pitted and soaked overnight in 1 cup of water

1 cup grain milk (see Hazelnut Hemp Mylk, page 28)

1/2 teaspoon vanilla

1 tablespoon lemon juice, optional

1/3 cup ice

Strain and rinse the cashews. Place all of the ingredients into a blender and purée on high until smooth and creamy. If the smoothie is too thick for your liking, just add a little more milk to the mixture. Pour into a large glass and enjoy.

Vegetable Juices

Fresh vegetable juice is one of the easiest ways to weave live enzymes and quality nutrients into our diet. Veggie juice is like a liquid salad. I often make a big glass of veggie juice for a light lunch because it is so easily digested and doesn't slow me down like a big meal can, especially on a hot day. There are many different kinds of vegetable juicers on the market and all will do the job. Choose a model that is within your budget and enjoy healthy freshly made juices at a fraction of the cost of store-bought.

The basic fresh vegetables used for juicing are: carrots, celery, beets, cucumbers, all leafy greens (lettuce, chard, kale, collards, spinach, parsley, cilantro, watercress, dandelion), and summer squash. Use bell pepper, broccoli, cauliflower, cabbage, turnip, radish, and fennel sparingly as their strong flavors can be overwhelming when juiced. Tomatoes are really a fruit, but can be added to make your juice taste like the classic V-8, but without the can. Apples and pears add a sweet note to these nutritious beverages, making them a little more kid friendly. Try adding a shot of freshly pressed wheat grass juice, a few cloves of garlic, a small chunk of ginger, or a whole lemon or lime to your favorite combination for added nutrients and flavorful accents. Use only the freshest vegetables, organically grown if at all possible, for making juice. Combine your favorite veggies and make your own blend or begin with one of the combinations below. Make fresh vegetable juice a part of your regular diet—it is time well spent and worth the extra effort for great flavor and vibrant health.

Carrot Cooler

MAKES 1 LARGE OR 2
SMALL SERVINGS

2 large carrots

4 stalks celery

1 whole cucumber, peeled
  if not organic

1 whole lime

Wash all vegetables well. Trim, if needed, and cut into pieces that will easily fit into your juicer. Juice all of the vegetables and drink immediately or store in refrigerator for 1–2 days.

Green Goodness

MAKES 1 LARGE OR 2
SMALL SERVINGS

4 large kale or chard leaves

2 stalks celery

Several sprigs of Italian
  parsley or cilantro

2 large carrots

Wash all vegetables well. Trim, if needed, and cut into pieces that will easily fit into your juicer. Juice all of the vegetables and drink immediately or store in refrigerator for 1–2 days.

Fennel Combo

MAKES 1 LARGE OR 2
SMALL SERVINGS

2 large carrots

1 medium-size beet

2 stalks celery

1 small bulb fennel

Wash all vegetables well. Trim, if needed, and cut into pieces that will easily fit into your juicer. Juice all of the vegetables and drink immediately or store in refrigerator for 1–2 days.

V-6

2 large carrots

1 small beet

2 stalks celery

1 large tomato

1 clove garlic

Large sprig of parsley

Wash all vegetables well. Trim, if needed, and cut into pieces that will easily fit into your juicer. Juice all of the vegetables and drink immediately or store in refrigerator for 1–2 days.

Spinach Cooler

1 bunch spinach, leaves and
   stems (approximately 6 cups)

1 whole cucumber, peeled
   if not organic

4 stalks celery

$1/2$-inch piece fresh gingerroot

Wash all vegetables well. Trim, if needed, and cut into pieces that will easily fit into your juicer. Juice all of the vegetables and drink immediately or store in refrigerator for 1–2 days.

Spicy Combo

**MAKES 1 LARGE OR 2
SMALL SERVINGS**

1 large carrot

1 medium-size red bell pepper

1 large tomato

1 small beet

1 cucumber, peeled if not organic

2 to 3 radishes

1 clove garlic

Several sprigs cilantro or parsley

Wash all vegetables well. Trim, if needed, and cut into pieces that will easily fit into your juicer. Juice all of the vegetables and drink immediately or store in refrigerator for 1–2 days.

When making a vegetable stock for soups and sauces use the vegetable fiber leftover from making the juice for a base. Place the pulp into a big stainless steel pot; add some chopped onions, and maybe a few herbs. Cover the vegetables with water, bring it all to a boil, turn down the heat and simmer for 30–40 minutes. For a quick and nutritious meal, strain out the vegetables, add a few fresh chopped veggies to the broth and cook until tender. Combine with miso and a little cooked rice or noodles for a simple, satisfying, and economical soup.

Hazelnut Hemp Mylk

MAKES 1 1/2 QUARTS

1/2 cup hazelnuts, soaked
 overnight in 2 cups water

3 dates, pitted and soaked in
 1/2 cup water for 1–2 hours

1/2 cup hemp seeds

Pinch of sea salt

4 to 6 cups fresh or filtered water,
 depending on desired thickness

Non-dairy "mylk" can be made from a wide variety of nuts, seeds, grains, and other whole foods. After you follow the recipe below and become familiar with the process, try making mylk with almonds, cashews, pistachios, or other nuts; sunflower, pumpkin, or sesame seeds; rice, oats, barley, or other grains and flavor with raisins, figs, coconut, cocoa, cinnamon, cardamom, vanilla, or whatever suites your taste.

Place the drained and rinsed hazelnuts, dates, hemp seeds, and salt into a blender. Secure the lid and blend on high for 1 minute. Add water in 1-cup increments, and blend for 2 minutes on high speed, or until smooth and creamy. Pour the mixture through a fine mesh sprouting bag* (see glossary) suspended over a bowl to catch the mylk and massage the bag until all that's left inside is dry pulp. Pour mylk into a glass and enjoy as is, chill, or serve with hot cereal.

* As an alternative, you can use a strainer lined with several layers of cheesecloth.

Hot Carob Cocoa

MAKES 4 SERVINGS

1 quart milk (whole dairy, grain, nut, or coconut)

2 tablespoons carob, cocoa, or cacao powder

4 to 5 pitted dates, depending on sweetness and size, or substitute ⅓ cup sucanat, honey, maple, or agave nectar, to taste

2 tablespoons barley malt

½ teaspoon vanilla

This recipe was inspired by the classic cookbook *Ten Talents* and has seen numerous variations in our kitchen, depending on what kind of milk or sweetener is used. The dates make this comforting beverage rich and satisfying, and blending the ingredients before and after you heat them is what gives the cocoa such a silky texture. For a special treat, top with freshly whipped cream, a drizzle of honey, and a sprinkle of cinnamon.

Place all the ingredients in a blender and liquefy on high speed until smooth and creamy. Pour into a saucepan and heat, but do not boil. Blend again, being careful of the heat, pour into mugs, and serve.

Green Tea Chai

MAKES 3-4 SERVINGS

3 cups boiling water

4 whole peppercorns

6 whole cardamom seeds

1 stick cinnamon, 2–3 inches long

1¼ teaspoons freshly grated nutmeg

1-inch piece fresh gingerroot, peeled and thinly sliced

3 to 4 tablespoons loose green tea or 4 tea bags

1 cup whole milk or Mylk (see Hazelnut Hemp Mylk, facing page) for a vegan version

1 to 2 tablespoons honey

In India, traditional chai is made with black tea, milk, and sugar, and the flavor is often too sweet for my taste. This remake uses antioxidant-rich green tea and a touch of honey for a healthy alternative. Adding a dash of vanilla or almond extract deepens the spice and adds a captivating aroma to this delicious version of chai.

Simmer water and spices for 15 minutes to infuse with flavor; add green tea, cover, and steep for several more minutes, depending on the strength you like.

In a small saucepan, gently heat the milk. Strain tea and spices and combine with the hot milk. Serve in big mugs and add honey or sweetener of choice, to taste.

Maté Latte

....

¼ cup loose Yerba Maté
   or 2 tea bags

3 cups hot, but not boiling water

1 cup warm whole milk or Mylk
   (see Hazelnut Hemp Mylk,
   page 28) for a vegan version

Honey, agave nectar, or sweetener
   of choice, optional

Yerba Maté has been used for generations by the indigenous people of South America as a natural source of energy and nutrition. Like other green teas that are wild harvested and cultivated in numerous cultures throughout the world, maté is rich in antioxidants and is a natural stimulant. This amazing herb is a good alternative to the daily coffee habit, and is much easier on our nervous system, stomach, and pocketbook.

Place the tea in a ceramic teapot or quart jar. Pour in water, cover, and steep 3–5 minutes, depending on desired strength.

In a small saucepan, heat the milk, but do not boil. Alternately, use a steamer in an espresso machine and heat the milk for a frothy latte finish. Strain tea into serving cups, add the warm milk, and sweeten to taste.

Morning Meals

Living Rise and Shine Granola

MAKES ABOUT 20 CUPS

1 cup raw sunflower seeds

1 cup raw pumpkin seeds

$1/2$ cup whole almonds

1 cup flax seeds

2 cups hulled buckwheat

$2/3$ cup chopped dates

$2/3$ cup maple syrup

1 cup fresh orange juice

1 tablespoon cinnamon

1 teaspoon cardamom

2 teaspoons sea salt

2 teaspoons vanilla

1 cup ground flax seeds

4 cups organic flaked grains
(such as a blend of oats, spelt,
barley, wheat, and kamut)

1 cup unsweetened coconut flakes

4 cups grated apple

1 cup plump raisins or soft-
textured dried fruit*

*Prunes, strawberries, raspberries,
blueberries, apples, apricots,
peaches, pears, nectarines,
figs, persimmons, mangos,
papaya, pineapple, kiwi, cherries,
bananas, or goji berries

This fantastic enzyme-rich granola is a favorite breakfast, snack, and travel food for my family. These crunchy clusters store well so we always make it in big batches. Unlike traditional baked and sugar-sweetened granolas, this recipe is made with whole seeds and grains that have been soaked, bringing them back to life, and uses natural sweeteners. The soaking and dehydrating process transforms these whole foods to develop flavor, ease digestion, and nourish us in a profound way. This delicious living granola is easy to prepare and costs a fraction of the expensive packaged breakfast cereals found on grocery store shelves and in the bulk bins of natural food stores.

Place the sunflower seeds, pumpkin seeds and almonds in separate bowls and pour 1 quart of water over each. Place the flax seeds in separate bowl, add 3 cups of water and stir. Place the buckwheat in a slightly larger bowl and add 2–3 quarts of water. Cover the bowls with a plate or clean cloths and leave to soak overnight.

In the morning, strain, drain, and rinse the sunflower seeds, pumpkin seeds, and almonds until the water runs clear. Chop the almonds into small pieces so they will dehydrate along with the other ingredients, and set aside. Rinse the gelatinous water from the buckwheat very well. This may take several cycles of rinsing and draining before the water is clear. Place all of the soaked ingredients, except the flax seeds, into a big strainer and set aside until ready to use.

Place the dates, maple syrup, orange juice, cinnamon, cardamom, salt, and vanilla in a blender and pulse to combine.

In a large mixing bowl, combine the ground flax, grains, coconut, apple, and raisins or dried fruit. Add the soaked flax seeds, including the gelatinous water, along with the sunflower and pumpkin seeds, buckwheat, and almonds. Using your hands, combine the mixture until all of the ingredients are evenly distributed throughout. Pour in the date mixture and massage into the grains and fruit to coat evenly.

If you have an electric or sun-powered dehydrator, by all means use it for this recipe, if not, see instructions for oven dehydrating on the next page. For electric dehydrators, spread the mixture evenly over several Teflex sheets, or use parchment paper, and dehydrate at 108 degrees F for 12–14 hours, or until thoroughly dry and crunchy.

If you choose to dehydrate your granola with sun power, use a well-sealed solar dehydrating unit that has good air circulation and will protect it from hungry critters.

Serve with yogurt and freshly cut seasonal fruit for a nutritious breakfast or enjoy by the handful as premium fuel for the body that will last throughout the day. Store in an airtight container for 1 month, or longer.

NOTE: *If the dried fruit is hard and leathery, soak the pieces in a small amount of water for several minutes, or up to 1 hour, to soften before using.*

OVEN DEHYDRATING METHOD:

Place the mixture in single layers on baking sheets lined with parchment paper and bake on the lowest temperature setting of your oven, preferably less than 110 degrees F, for 10–12 hours, or until thoroughly dry and crunchy. Most gas ovens stay around 100 degrees F from the residual heat that comes from the pilot light and this will work just fine for the recipe. If you are using an electric oven, keep the temperature as low as possible to retain the live enzymes and check with an accurate thermometer if in doubt. If your oven has convection setting, use it because the moving air will speed the drying process, if not, keep the door slightly ajar to encourage air circulation.

Live Oat and Tropical Fruit Muesli

....

¹/₄ cup oat groats

¹/₄ cup whole almonds

1 tablespoon hulled sunflower seeds

1 tablespoon hulled pumpkin seeds

1 banana, cut into ¹/₂-inch rounds

¹/₂ cup fresh pineapple, cut into ³/₄-inch chunks

¹/₂ cup fresh papaya or mango, cut into ³/₄-inch chunks

1 tablespoon agave nectar

1 teaspoon lemon juice

OPTIONAL ADDITIONS FOR ADDED NUTRITION AND FLAVOR:

¹/₂ cup freshly squeezed orange juice or a whole peeled orange, seeds removed

¹/₃ cup Yogurt (page 141)

1 tablespoon flax seed oil

1 tablespoon bee pollen

Maca root powder

Live muesli is a morning staple of the Esalen Staff Cleanse and a different version of this nourishing, simple, and quick-to-prepare breakfast is served in the lodge at least once a week. Soaking the oats, nuts, and seeds overnight removes the enzyme inhibitors and transforms them into a living food, making these naturally sweet morsels much easier for our body to digest. I admit that I am terribly fond of bananas and eat them at home, as well as in the tropics, but locally grown seasonal fruit is always the best choice for your morning muesli. Substitute local fruits whenever possible and enjoy live muesli as an enzyme-rich and satisfying breakfast that will fuel a long hard day's work with sound nutrition.

Place the oats, nuts, and seeds in 2 cups water and soak overnight. When you're ready to eat, drain off the soaking water, rinse the oats, nuts, and seeds well. Strain and drain again before placing them in a large clean bowl. Add the banana, pineapple, and papaya or mango.

In a separate small bowl, blend the agave nectar and lemon juice along with any optional additions. Pour the agave nectar mixture into the bowl, stir to combine, and serve.

Perfect Oatmeal

....

1³/₄ cups water

1 cup rolled oats

Pinch of salt, optional

When I first began to cook breakfast at Esalen, a long-time supervisor on the maintenance crew, who ate a bowl of oatmeal every day, came into the kitchen one morning and told me that the oatmeal was perfect. Now perfect for some folks is to stir the oatmeal into a glue-like consistency, but for this person, the cover and leave alone method which leaves the gluten in the grain was what he preferred. So do I. When shopping, look for thick organic rolled oats because they tend to be more flavorful and have better texture than the other varieties.

In a saucepan with a tight-fitting lid, bring the water to a boil, stir in oats, and salt, if using. Cover and cook over low heat for 20 minutes. For the best texture, do not lift the lid or stir the oatmeal before it is finished cooking. To keep the grains light and fluffy, do not stir the oatmeal in the pot, just spoon it into serving bowls and embellish with maple syrup, fresh or dried fruit, dairy, nut or grain milk, and a little cinnamon. For a savory change, try it topped with butter, tamari, nutritional yeast, and a sprinkle of pumpkin seeds.

DRIED FRUIT VARIATION:

Bring the water to a boil, add raisins or bite-sized pieces of dried apples, pears, peaches, apricots, nectarines, figs, or dates and bring the water back to a boil. Stir in the oats and follow the directions above.

Brown Rice Cream with Dates, Cinnamon, and Vanilla

MAKES 4 SERVINGS

1 cup ground brown rice

4 cups water, more or less, depending on the grind of the grain

1/3 cup dates, pitted and chopped small

1/2 to 1 teaspoon ground cinnamon

1/2 teaspoon vanilla

Porridge, mush, and gruel are good words to describe the texture of brown rice cream. Smooth and satisfying, rice cream is a perfect first cereal for babies—simple, sweet, and nutritious. In this recipe, toasting the grain before cooking develops the nutty flavor that makes this creamy textured hot cereal so flavorful. For a change of pace, omit the dates, cinnamon, and vanilla and embellish with any of your favorite sweet or savory toppings and use it like any other cooked grain.

To make brown rice cream, grind rice in a food mill/coffee grinder in small batches. Place the ground rice into a large skillet and toast over medium heat until fragrant, 3–5 minutes.

Slowly pour the water into the rice, whisking as you go to keep the texture lump-free and creamy, until you have a smooth consistency. Stir in the dates, cinnamon, and vanilla and simmer over low heat for 15–20 minutes. Stir often and add small increments of water as needed to keep from scorching.

SPICED VARIATION:
Add a little fresh grated nutmeg or ginger, a pinch of ground cardamom or cloves, and a generous sprinkling of cinnamon.

Breakfast Quinoa with Fresh Strawberries, Blueberries, and Almonds

MAKES 4 SERVINGS

1¾ cups water

1 cup organic quinoa, rinsed thoroughly and drained

Pinch of salt, optional

1 cup sliced fresh strawberries, divided

1 cup fresh blueberries, divided

⅓ cup chopped almonds

YOGURT SAUCE

1 cup Yogurt (page 141)

¼ cup agave nectar

Quinoa is a nutritious foundation for both sweet and savory additions. When you're short on time, try quinoa as a convenient substitution for rice or pasta, top with sautéed or steamed vegetables, your favorite sauce, and bit of grated cheese for a quick and nutritious dish.

Quinoa is a perfect breakfast grain. It cooks quickly, is high in protein, and has a light texture that adds a wonderful little crunch to each bite. This seasonal recipe features fresh strawberries, blueberries, and agave nectar-sweetened yogurt for a delicious summer breakfast.

Using a medium-size saucepan that has a tight-fitting lid, bring the water to a boil. Add the quinoa and salt, cover, lower the heat, and simmer for 12–15 minutes, or until all the water is absorbed. When the quinoa is fully cooked, fluff the grains and spoon into serving bowls. Top with ¼ cup each strawberries and blueberries and garnish with almonds. Combine the Yogurt and agave nectar in a small bowl and serve the sauce on the side.

Dried Fruit Compote

MAKES 4 CUPS

2 cups organic dried fruit, chopped into bite-size pieces (such as apples, apricots, peaches, pears, prunes, nectarines, figs, persimmons, mangos, papaya, and pineapple)

$\frac{1}{4}$ cup honey or agave nectar, more or less depending on the sweetness of the fruit

1 lemon, cut in half crosswise and seeded

1 small orange, cut in quarters and seeded

1 (3-inch) stick cinnamon

5 whole cloves

3 pods coriander, optional

Compotes awaken the flavors of dried fruit that has been picked at its peak and dehydrated, brightening a cold winter day with the memories of summer's warmth. For the best flavor, and to avoid unwanted chemical residue, I recommend you use organically grown and sulfur-free fruit whenever possible. Serve this compote with your favorite hot cereal grain for a hearty and nutritious breakfast, or spoon warm compote over vanilla ice cream and top with chopped nuts for a simple dessert.

Place all ingredients in a medium-size saucepan, cover with 1 inch water, then cover pan with a tight-fitting lid and simmer for 20–30 minutes, or until fruit is soft and thickens the water into a syrup. If you cook the mixture longer, the fruit will begin to loose shape and your compote will take on a more jam-like consistency. When the compote is done to your liking, set aside to cool. When you are ready to use, remove the citrus and spices, and serve alone or over breakfast grains, ice cream, yogurt, or pancakes as a nutritious and naturally sweet topping. Store in refrigerator for up to 1 week, or can in jars and store in a cool larder.

Bali Toast

2 eggs

$1/2$ cup plain Yogurt (page 141)

1 fully ripe banana

$1/2$ cup whole dairy, grain, or nut milk

$1/2$ teaspoon cinnamon

$1/2$ teaspoon vanilla

2 tablespoons coconut oil

6 slices whole grain bread

$1/4$ cup unsalted butter

$1/2$ cup pure maple syrup

This version of French toast dresses up the traditional breakfast with a tropical twist and whole grain goodness. While traveling in Bali with my young children, the local women used to make us these strange looking flat pancakes with thin slices of banana cooked into them—but they tasted really good. Everyone in our family loves the flavor of sweet ripe bananas, and, when we returned home, the kids and I created this recipe. The whole grain bread is infused with the flavor of those Bali pancakes, yogurt gives it a tang, and the cinnamon adds a finishing spice to this yummy breakfast treat. For a special Sunday brunch, top Bali Toast with sliced papaya, mango, or strawberries and a dollop of maple-sweetened yogurt, or simply serve with unsalted butter and maple syrup for a quick and hearty breakfast.

In a medium-size mixing bowl, beat the eggs and Yogurt until creamy. Mash the banana in a separate bowl and add the milk, cinnamon, and vanilla and then stir. Pour the banana mixture into the eggs and briskly whisk together, mashing any pieces as you go to blend them into the liquid.

Heat a griddle or iron skillet over medium-high heat and add the coconut oil. Dip the bread slices into the egg mixture, coat both sides completely, and cook the pieces for several minutes on each side until golden brown. Place on warm plates and top with butter and maple syrup.

Multigrain Blueberry Pancakes

2$\frac{1}{2}$ cups whole wheat or
    spelt pastry flour

$\frac{1}{3}$ cup corn flour

$\frac{1}{3}$ cup rolled oats

1 tablespoon baking powder

2 teaspoons baking soda

1 teaspoon sea salt

$\frac{1}{4}$ cup sucanat

5 eggs, separated

3 cups buttermilk

$\frac{1}{4}$ cup melted Ghee (page 150)

1$\frac{1}{2}$ cups fresh blueberries, divided

A lot of solid nutrition can be packed into a pancake when made with a variety of flavorful whole grains, fresh eggs, and sweet buttermilk. Whipping the egg whites separately and folding them in at the last minute keeps these tasty cakes light and moist. Making your own whole-grain pancake mix is considerably less expensive than the packaged kind and is quick and simple to do. Mix the dry ingredients together and store in an airtight jar with a tight-fitting lid. On a busy morning just add the wet ingredients, mix, and cook for a quick and nourishing breakfast, with or without the blueberries.

In a large mixing bowl, mix the dry ingredients together and set aside. In small mixing bowl, beat the egg yolks, buttermilk, and Ghee.

In a separate bowl, beat the egg whites until stiff, but not dry. Using a wooden spoon or rubber spatula, combine the egg yolk mixture with the dry ingredients in a few swift strokes. Carefully fold in 1 cup blueberries and the egg whites without breaking too many of the bubbles. For the best texture, do not over mix the batter. Ladle about $\frac{1}{3}$ cup batter onto a lightly greased medium-hot griddle and cook for 3–4 minutes. Carefully flip the cakes over when bubbles appear on top and the bottom is golden brown. Continue cooking on the other side for 2–3 minutes or until done. Top hot pancakes with whipped butter, real maple syrup, and garnish with the reserved blueberries. Double wrap and freeze any extra pancakes. Heat in a warm oven when ready to serve.

Blueberries are a nutritional goldmine. These sweet little balls of blue are high in antioxidants, fiber, and vitamin C. Low on the Glycemic Index; blueberries are an important consideration for those looking to lower their intake of refined or natural sugars. Wild blueberries tend to be smaller in size than the commercially grown varieties and are well worth the effort to forage if you live in a place where they grow. For the freshest commercially grown blueberries at the best price, look to your local farmers market during the months of May through October. Blueberries freeze very well, so stock up on them in season and pack into your freezer for a little taste of summer on a cold winter day.

Sourdough Buckwheat Pancakes

MAKES 4 SERVINGS

2 cups Sourdough Starter
(page 157)

2 eggs, beaten

2 tablespoon melted Ghee
(page 150)

3 tablespoons honey

$1/2$ teaspoon vanilla

$1/2$ teaspoon sea salt

1 cup buckwheat flour

$1/2$ to 1 cup whole wheat pastry
flour, depending on the
consistency of starter

$1/2$ teaspoon baking soda

Sourdough starter must be tended and used often to keep it growing and ready for bread making. Sourdough pancakes are another wonderful way to incorporate your precious starter, especially when you don't have the time to make bread. Buckwheat flour has an earthy mild flavor and blends perfectly with the tang of sourdough to make these hearty cakes.

In a large mixing bowl, combine the starter, eggs, Ghee, honey, and vanilla and mix well.

Add the salt, flours, and baking soda and mix together with a few swift strokes until just combined. The batter will be thick or thin depending on the consistency of your starter. Add a little more flour or water as needed so that it will pour smoothly without being too runny. Ladle the batter onto a lightly greased medium-hot griddle and cook until bubbles appear on the top and the bottom is golden brown, about 3–4 minutes. With a large spatula, carefully flip the pancakes over and cook the other side for an additional 2–3 minutes, or until the center is done.

Serve pancakes hot and top with unsalted butter, warm maple syrup, sliced fresh seasonal fruit or Dried Fruit Compote (page 38) for a hearty and nutritious breakfast.

Scrambled Tofu and Fresh Veggies

MAKES 4 SERVINGS

1 pound firm tofu

1 tablespoon extra virgin olive oil

1 tablespoon Ghee (page 150),
    optional for added flavor

1/3 cup finely chopped carrot

1/3 cup finely chopped
    red bell pepper

1/2 cup sliced shiitake or button
    mushrooms, optional

1/2 teaspoon turmeric

1 teaspoon Dijon mustard

1 tablespoon tamari

1 teaspoon Bragg's liquid
    aminos, optional

1 to 2 tablespoons nutritional yeast

1/4 teaspoon sea salt

Freshly ground pepper

2 cups fresh spinach, roughly
    chopped or whole baby leaves

1/3 cup finely sliced green onions

2 tablespoons finely chopped
    Italian parsley

1 tablespoon chopped fresh
    basil or 1/2 teaspoon dried

2 teaspoons chopped fresh
    oregano or 1/2 teaspoon dried

1 teaspoon finely chopped fresh
    sage or rosemary, optional

Gomasio (page 149)

Scrambled tofu is a hearty vegan breakfast, lunch, or dinner that non-vegans can enjoy as a low-fat alternative to eggs—a welcome dish for those looking to limit their cholesterol intake. In this recipe the seasonings are absorbed into the sautéed tofu and perfectly balance the flavors of fresh vegetables and herbs. Ground turmeric gives the tofu a rich golden hue, and with the bright colors of the fresh veggies, this dish is visually stunning. For a quick and easy meal serve with whole grain toast and a tomato-cucumber salad on the side. This savory scramble also tastes great piled on top of cooked grains or tossed with rice noodles and your favorite grated cheese for a nutritious meal.

Rinse and drain tofu and then press in a towel to remove excess water. If the tofu still has a lot of water in it, weight with a can or something else clean and heavy for at least 20 minutes to squeeze out the excess liquid. Crumble the tofu after the water is removed.

In a large skillet, heat oil and Ghee, if using. Sauté carrots and bell pepper for 2–3 minutes over medium-high heat. Add the mushrooms and cook for another 3–4 minutes. Add the drained and crumbled tofu and cook for 6–8 minutes, stirring frequently until all the moisture is absorbed and the tofu begins to set.

While the tofu is cooking, mix together the turmeric, mustard, tamari, aminos, yeast, salt, and pepper in a small bowl. Stir the paste into the tofu mixture, cover, and cook for another 2–3 minutes, stirring a couple of times for the flavors to bloom. Mix in the spinach, onions, and herbs; cover and continue cooking until all the spinach is wilted, about 1–2 minutes. Serve with a sprinkle of Gomasio.

Huevos Rancheros

2 to 4 tablespoons
 coconut oil, divided

1 large onion, halved
 and thinly sliced

1 large pasilla pepper, halved,
 seeded, and thinly sliced, or
 substitute green bell pepper

1 jalapeño, minced, optional

1 tablespoon minced garlic

1/2 teaspoon toasted and
 ground cumin seed

3 cups chopped tomatoes

1/2 cup vegetable stock

1 cup refried or seasoned
 whole beans (or Chipotle
 Black Beans, page 106)

8 eggs

2 tablespoons coconut oil

8 Corn Tortillas (page 154)

1 cup crumbled queso fresco
 or grated Monterey Jack
 cheese (about 1/4 pound)

1/4 cup chopped cilantro

I have enjoyed this dish on many a trip south of the border and discovered that Huevos Rancheros has as many variations as there are cooks in Mexico. This fresh and simple version can be made quickly with just a few basic ingredients, and the beautiful presentation is perfect for special occasions. If you prefer a smooth sauce, blend the vegetables before pouring over the eggs—either way this is a wonderful tasting, nutritious, and very economical traditional Mexican dish. Serve with sliced avocado, a green salad, or rice, and a basket of hot tortillas on the side for breakfast, brunch, lunch, or supper.

Place 2 tablespoons coconut oil in a heavy skillet, add the onion, and sauté until translucent. Add peppers, garlic, and cumin and cook for 2–3 minutes. Add the tomatoes and cook over medium-high heat, deglazing the skillet with stock as necessary to keep the veggies from sticking. Add the remaining stock and simmer for 10 minutes, or until the sauce thickens and the vegetables are tender.

If you are using whole beans, pulse in a food processor until they resemble the texture of traditional refried beans. Place the refried or puréed beans in a heavy saucepan, cover, and gently heat, stirring often to keep from scorching. A double boiler is useful for this step.

Gently poach the eggs in simmering water, or fry in a little coconut oil, until they are done to your liking.

I like my tortillas soft and oil free and I heat them in a heavy skillet or griddle just before the eggs are done to keep them nice and hot. If you prefer crispy tortillas, massage a small amount of coconut or vegetable oil on each side and heat in a 350-degree F oven for 3–6 minutes, or until the tortillas are hot and crispy. You can also fry the tortillas in hot oil and drain on paper towels before proceeding to the next step.

Place 2 tortillas on each plate and spread with 1/4 cup beans, top with the cooked eggs, and spoon the veggies and sauce over all. Sprinkle generously with cheese, garnish with cilantro, and serve hot.

Amphora Eggs Benedict

MAKES 4 SERVINGS

HOLLANDAISE SAUCE

5 fresh egg yolks

2 tablespoons fresh lemon juice

1 tablespoon fresh lime juice or
   substitute more lemon juice

1 cup melted Ghee (page 150)

1 teaspoon Sriracha

$1/2$ teaspoon sea salt

Freshly ground white pepper, to taste

8 eggs

4 English muffins, use the
   Sourdough English Muffin
   (page 162) or Honey Whole
   Grain Bread (page 164)

TOPPING OPTIONS

8 thick slices Canadian bacon,
   ham, or turkey, heated

8 slices smoked salmon

2 cups fresh crab meat,
   steamed warm

2 ripe avocados, sliced

8 thick slices fresh tomato,
   very lightly sautéed in a little
   unsalted butter or Ghee with
   a few chopped green onions

4 cups sliced mushrooms, sautéed
   in a little unsalted butter or Ghee

8 cups fresh spinach, wilted

2 cups Chipotle Black
   Beans (page 106)

1 whole fire-roasted sweet pepper,
   peeled and sliced into thin strips

The Café Amphora at Nepenthe was known up and down the Big Sur coast for serving awesome Eggs Benedict made with several variations on the traditional theme. Our distinctive Benedicts were made with whole grain muffins topped with a variety of flavorful fillings. Gently poached eggs were nested on the filling and our famous Hollandaise sauce was generously poured over the top. When making Hollandaise sauce and poaching eggs, use only very fresh, preferably organic and free-range, eggs for the best results. Eggs Benedict is really quite simple to make, it just takes a bit of planning and good timing. With a little practice and the tips in the recipe below, you can easily master this dish and serve it for an elegant brunch or special occasion to the delight of friends and family.

TO MAKE THE HOLLANDAISE BY HAND:

In a medium stainless steel bowl whisk egg yolks, lemon juice, and lime juice together until smooth. Continue whisking while gradually adding melted Ghee in a steady stream and the sauce becomes thick and silky. Blend in the Srirachi, salt, and pepper. Adjust the seasoning to taste with a little hot sauce, lemon juice, salt, or pepper.

TO MAKE THE HOLLANDAISE WITH A BLENDER:

Put all ingredients, except the Ghee, into a blender. With the speed on low, add the Ghee in a slow steady stream, until it is all incorporated into the sauce. If you are making a large batch and multiplying this recipe, you may need to add a little warm water, in 1 tablespoon increments, to keep your blender flowing until all the butter is incorporated. The sauce will be fine, just a little lighter in color and texture.

The eggs must be very fresh and cold for poaching. In a wide shallow stainless steel pan or skillet, bring between 2–3 inches of water to a boil and reduce to simmering. Carefully break the eggs one at a time into the water, giving the egg a little twist as you drop them in to wrap the white around the yolk. If you are not sure of the freshness of your eggs, or the whites are having trouble hanging on to the yolk, add 1 tablespoon vinegar to the water. Adding vinegar tends to change the texture and can toughen the eggs, so I only use if needed.

While the eggs are cooking, split the English muffins in half and toast on both sides. Put two halves per serving on warmed plates; place the topping of choice on each muffin half.

When the eggs are done to your liking, about 3–5 minutes, gently remove from the water with a slotted spoon. Pause the spoon on a clean towel to let the excess water drain and carefully place the eggs on the topped muffins. Pour ¼ cup warm Hollandaise sauce over each egg, sprinkle with a little paprika, and serve hot.

Samurai Breakfast

MAKES 4 SERVINGS

4 eggs

Salt and pepper, to taste

4 tablespoons coconut oil, Ghee (page 150), or vegetable oil of choice, divided

3 cups cooked short-grain brown rice

$1/4$ cup water

$1/4$ cup thinly sliced green onions

1 large avocado, peeled and sliced

$1/4$ cup raw sunflower seeds, dehydrated (page 147) or Tamari-Toasted (page 147)

This traditional Japanese breakfast is savory, not sweet, and rice is usually served in a variety of ways. The Samurai breakfast is not really a recipe, but a core meal in our home that we enjoy morning, noon, and night with numerous variations on the theme. With leftover cooked grain in the refrigerator, this savory and nutritious dish can be made in just a few minutes, a blessing when you're pressed for time and want a wholesome breakfast. For a change of pace, add sautéed vegetables, grated cheese, or sprouts to the mixture and nest poached eggs on the top instead of scrambling them into the rice. This is a deeply nourishing dish that calls to be embellished with the ethnic flavors of pesto, salsa, ponzu, or your favorite seasonings.

Break eggs into a small bowl, whisk with salt and pepper and set aside. Place 2 tablespoons coconut oil in a steel wok or heavy skillet over medium heat, add the brown rice and toss with a stainless steel wok spatula or wooden spoon, coating the grains evenly with oil. Add the water, cover, and cook for 3–4 minutes, stirring several times to keep the rice from sticking to the bottom until it is hot.

Remove the lid and stir in the green onions. Push the rice up the sides of the wok, or to the outside of the skillet, making a well in center and place the remaining 2 tablespoons oil in the middle. Pour in the eggs and cook gently, trying not to mix too much of the egg into the rice until they are set. When the eggs are cooked to your liking, quickly stir in the rice. Spoon into bowls and top with slices of avocado and sunflower seeds. Pass the tamari, nutritional yeast, Gomasio, dulse, ground flax seeds, or other seasoning of choice to sprinkle on top.

Soups, Sauces,
and Gravies

Stock

All good soups begin with a flavorful stock. The superior flavor of freshly made vegetable stock is well worth the extra time and will dramatically improve the flavor of all your soups and sauces. A simmering stock fills the kitchen with warmth, a wonderful aroma, and the promise of a comforting meal that is both nourishing and delicious. Begin with the basics: onions, carrots, and celery, and add other vegetables like potatoes, leeks, mushrooms, corn cobs, tomatoes, garlic, greens, squash, and herbs depending on the season and the kind of soup you are making. Starchier vegetables tend to make the finished stock a bit cloudy, which is not a problem for most uses, but if you want a clear broth you might choose to omit them. Vegetables in the Brassica family such as cabbage, broccoli, turnips, and cauliflower tend to give the finished stock a strong flavor and must be used sparingly, or not at all. The veggies can also be enriched with fish, fowl/poultry, or meat bones for added flavor and a nutritional boost. Making a fresh stock is really very easy. Begin with this simple recipe and adjust the ingredients to suit your personal tastes and the seasonal offerings as you build your skills in the fine art and tradition of soup making.

Fresh Vegetable Stock

MAKES 1 GALLON

3 large onions, chopped

2 to 3 cloves garlic, crushed

2 large leeks, sliced lengthwise, rinsed well, and cut into 1-inch pieces

2 large potatoes, cut into 2-inch chunks

4 large carrots, cut into 1-inch chunks

6 ribs celery, cut into 1-inch chunks

$1/3$ cup dried shiitake mushrooms or $1/2$ cup chopped fresh mushrooms

2 to 3 corn cobs, with corn kernels removed, and broken into pieces, optional

2 to 3 large tomatoes, chopped

$1/2$ cup chopped parsley, with stems

6 whole peppercorns

2 fresh bay leaves or 1 dried leaf

Bouquet garni, optional

4 to 5 quarts cold water

Place all the ingredients into a large soup pot, making sure there is enough water to cover the vegetables. Cover the pot with a tight-fitting lid and bring to a boil. Lower the heat and simmer for approximately 1 hour to infuse the flavor of the vegetables into the water. Strain the vegetables by pouring the broth through a sieve or mesh strainer, saving the rich broth in another pot or bowl below.

NOTE: *If you are using bones in your stock, cook for 2 hours and skim the fat and foam off the top before using. Use stock immediately, or store in the refrigerator for 5–6 days. Fresh stock can be cooled and frozen in different size containers, from ice cube trays up to 5-gallon buckets, and be ready and waiting for you when inspiration strikes.*

ROASTED STOCK VARIATION:

For special occasions, or when you have the extra time, roasting the fresh vegetables before they are boiled adds another dimension to the flavor of your stock, and is very easy to do. In a large ovenproof pan, combine the cut fresh vegetables, and bones if using, and roast in a 300-degree F oven for 45 minutes to 1 hour. Remove pan from the oven, place the vegetables into a large soup pot, cover with water, and proceed with making the stock as directed above. This technique produces darker colored broth and the roasted vegetables develop a sweetness that deepens the flavor of soups, sauces, and gravies.

Basic Vegetable Soup

1¹⁄₂ cups chopped onions

2 tablespoons extra virgin olive oil

1 cup sliced leeks, rinsed well

1 cup sliced celery

1 cup sliced carrots

¹⁄₂ cup chopped potato

1 to 2 cups bite-size pieces
    seasonal vegetables (see
    list on facing page)

¹⁄₂ cup sliced mushrooms

1 to 2 tablespoons minced garlic

8 cups vegetable stock

¹⁄₂ cup chopped fresh tomato or
    2 tablespoons tomato paste

2 cups chopped tender greens,
    spinach, chard, or collards

3 tablespoons chopped
    Italian parsley

2 tablespoons fresh chopped
    basil or 1 tablespoon dried

1 tablespoon fresh chopped
    thyme or 1 teaspoon dried

1 tablespoon fresh chopped
    oregano or 1 teaspoon dried

1 teaspoon sea salt

Freshly ground white pepper,
    to taste

There are a few tricks for making a flavorful vegetable soup, the richness of the stock being the most important component. After making a beautiful stock, I look to the garden veggies calling out to be picked or the beautiful displays at the farmers market to inspire me. Cutting the vegetables into different shapes and sizes will ensure that each one is perfectly cooked, and sautéing them in a little oil seals the edges and helps the pieces hold their shape in the broth. Deglazing the bottom of the pan with just a little stock adds richness to the soup by infusing the broth with the sugars released from the cooking vegetables.

For a more substantial soup, add cooked beans or grains, and garnish with a bit of cheese to boost the nutritional value and make it a complete meal. Making soup from scratch offers us the opportunity to be inventive and economical by using the odds and ends of vegetables, whether from the garden or the bottom of the refrigerator.

In a big soup pot over medium-high heat, sauté the onions in oil until translucent. Before the onions begin to brown, add the leeks and cook for 2–3 minutes. Add the celery, carrots, potato, and any dense seasonal vegetable to the pot and cook, stirring often, for 6–8 minutes, or until the vegetables begin to soften. The timing on the cooking of the vegetables will depend on the shapes and how big or little each one was cut. The trick is to put the firmer textured vegetables such as carrots, potatoes, and turnips into the pot first, adding each one at just the right time so that they will be done to perfection.

When the firmer veggies are al dente, add the mushrooms, garlic, and quick cooking seasonal veggies, like sliced zucchini or asparagus, to the pot and sauté for another 3–4 minutes, or until vegetables are lightly cooked. To deepen the flavor of your soup, slowly deglaze the pot with stock, adding only ¹⁄₄ cup at a time, until the caramelized sugars stuck on the bottom are released into the broth. Add the tomato, greens, herbs, seasonings, and the remaining stock and simmer for several minutes, cooking the vegetables to your liking. Adjust the seasoning with a little more salt and pepper if needed.

SEASONAL VEGETABLES

....

SPRING:

Asparagus

Cabbage

Greens

Peas

SUMMER:

Beans

Bell peppers

Corn

Eggplant

Okra

Peas

Potatoes

Tomatoes

FALL:

Cauliflower

Squash

Sweet potatoes

Peppers

Greens

WINTER:

Beets

Broccoli

Brussels sprouts

Potatoes

Rutabagas

Turnips

Winter squash

Miso Vegetable Soup

....

1/4 cup wakame or arame
  seaweed, optional

2 tablespoons unrefined sesame
  or light vegetable oil

1 tablespoon toasted sesame oil

1/4 cup minced shallots

1 tablespoon minced garlic

1 tablespoon grated gingerroot

1/3 cup very thinly sliced or
  matchstick-cut carrots

1/3 cup diagonally sliced celery

1/3 cup sliced snow peas

2 teaspoons dashi, omit
  for vegan version

1 teaspoon shiitake mushroom
  powder, optional

4 cups vegetable stock
  or water, divided

1/2 pound tofu, cut into 1/2-
  inch cubes, optional

1/3 to 1/2 cup miso

1/3 cup thinly sliced green
  onion, rings separated

1/4 cup chopped cilantro

Miso is made in many different styles and the darker the color, the saltier the taste—a trademark of this versatile and nutritious food. Most miso comes in either a red, brown, or white paste, and I encourage you to explore them all. Begin with a mellow white, barley, or red miso and be sure to try one of the more unique variations.

This recipe is a vegetarian version of a classic simple soup that has been a staple of the Japanese for centuries, and is still an integral part of their diet today.

Place seaweed in small bowl and cover with warm water to rehydrate for at least 10 minutes.

Heat the oils in a large soup pot; add the shallots, and sauté until translucent. Add the garlic, gingerroot, carrots, and celery and any other firm seasonal vegetable (see list below), and cook for 2–3 minutes Add the snow peas and more delicate seasonal vegetables (see list below), stir in the dashi and mushroom powder, if using, and cook for 2–3 minutes to deepen the flavors.

Deglaze the bottom of the pot by adding the stock in small increments, reserving 1 cup. Add the seaweed, with soaking water, and the tofu to the soup pot, cover, and heat. With a small whisk or a fork, blend the miso into the reserved cup of stock until smooth. When the soup is just about to boil, remove from heat and stir in the miso mixture. Ladle the soup into warm bowls and garnish with green onions and cilantro.

NOTE: *If you reheat this soup, remember not to boil it so the healthy enzymes in the miso remain intact.*

SEASONAL VARIATIONS:

Use approximately 1/2 cup, or more or less to taste, of your choice of thinly sliced or diced fresh mushrooms; sweet peppers, all kinds; green, Napa, or Chinese cabbage; bok choy; leeks; chopped or baby spinach; chard; kale; butternut squash; green beans; daikon; potatoes; yams; snow peas; mung bean sprouts

Indonesian Chicken Soup

STOCK

1 whole chicken, about 3 to 4 pounds, cut into quarters

8 cups cold water

1 cup chopped onion

1/2 cup each chopped celery and carrot

1 (2-inch piece) gingerroot, sliced into 1/4-inch rounds

1 tablespoon minced lemongrass

2 to 4 kaffir lime leaves

SOUP

1 tablespoon unrefined sesame oil

1 cup chopped shallots or onions

1 tablespoon minced garlic

1 tablespoon minced gingerroot

1 tablespoon minced lemongrass

1 teaspoon minced fresh jalapeño

1 teaspoon sea salt

1/2 cup matchstick-cut carrots

1/2 cup thinly sliced zucchini

1/3 cup thinly sliced celery

1/4 cup thinly sliced red bell pepper

1 cup sliced bok choy

1/2 cup diagonally sliced fresh snow peas

1/2 pound rice noodles, cooked al dente according to directions

2 cups chopped spinach

2 tablespoons tamari or Bragg's liquid aminos

Pinch or two of cayenne, optional

1/3 cup chopped cilantro

1/3 cup sliced scallions

1 fresh lime, cut into wedges

In this recipe, the chicken stock is enriched with circulation-stimulating spices, nutrient-rich veggies and fresh flavors from the Far East, making this a perfect warming soup for a cold winter's day. Chicken soup has been a traditional medicine used for generations, and each culture has own their unique way of putting it all together. With the addition of your time, effort, and love, this recipe will nourish and comfort dear ones who are under the weather and help them regain their strength. This is one of those soups that everyone in the family appreciates, even when they are feeling perfectly healthy.

Place the stock ingredients in a large soup pot and cook on medium high heat until it just begins to boil. Lower the heat and simmer for 50–60 minutes, or until the meat begins to fall from the bones, stirring occasionally. Remove chicken from the stock, cool, and separate the meat from the bones and skin. Tear the chicken into bite-size pieces, cover, and set aside. Return the bones to the soup pot and continue to simmer the broth while you prepare the soup vegetables.

To make the soup, pour the sesame oil into a large soup pot over medium-high heat; add the shallots and sauté for 2 minutes. When the shallots begin to look translucent, add the garlic, gingerroot, lemongrass, jalapeño, and sea salt and cook for 1–2 minutes, stirring constantly to keep from scorching. Stir in the carrots, zucchini, celery, and bell pepper and sauté for 1–2 minutes. Add the bok choy, snow peas, mung beans, and chicken meat and bring the soup back up to a simmer. Stir in the cooked noodles, spinach, and tamari and continue simmering until the spinach has wilted. Adjust the seasoning with a little more sea salt or tamari and cayenne to taste. Ladle into bowls and garnish with cilantro, scallions, and a wedge of lime.

Fusion Lentil Soup with Basil and Cashew Pesto

MAKES 4–6 SERVINGS

2 tablespoons extra virgin olive oil

1 cup chopped onion

$1/2$ cup sliced celery

$1/2$ cup sliced carrot

$1/2$ cup sliced zucchini or other summer squash

$1/4$ cup chopped fennel

$1/4$ cup chopped red bell pepper

1 large bay leaf

$1^1/2$ cups dried lentils, picked through and rinsed

$2^1/2$ quarts vegetable stock or water, divided

$1/2$ cup chopped tomato

2 teaspoons chopped garlic

$1^1/2$ teaspoons sea salt

1 teaspoon Bragg's liquid aminos or tamari

2 tablespoons fresh chopped basil

3 tablespoons chopped fresh Italian parsley

Pinch of cayenne or freshly ground pepper, to taste

1 cup Basil Cashew Pesto (see Garden Pesto, page 136)

Lentil soup can be made in any number of ways, and this recipe is a fusion of French, Mediterranean, and Middle Eastern cuisine. It has a rich and earthy flavor that can be varied to incorporate a wide variety of different vegetables, depending on the season, or what ever is calling to be harvested from the garden when you're ready to make soup. In this recipe, the fresh vegetables are bathed in a rich lentil-infused stock and finished with a dollop of basil and cashew pesto for a hearty and satisfying soup. You can use either the delicate French green lentil or the larger brown lentils found in most grocery stores as both will work fine.

In a heavy-bottom soup pot, heat the oil and sauté the onion for 5 minutes, or until translucent. Add the celery, carrot, zucchini, fennel, and bell pepper and continue cooking for 2–3 minutes, stirring constantly to keep from scorching. Add the bay leaf and lentils and deglaze the pot with $1/2$ cup vegetable stock. Pour in the remaining stock and stir. You may need to add a little more liquid as the lentils cook, depending on their size. Cover the pot and simmer for 40–50 minutes, or until the lentils are tender.

Add the tomato, garlic, salt, and aminos, and simmer for another 10 minutes to marry the flavors. Stir in the basil and parsley, taste, and adjust the seasoning with a little more salt and pepper, if needed. Garnish with a dollop of Basil Cashew Pesto and serve with warm bread and a fresh green salad.

Sunshine Yam Soup

SERVES 4–6

½ cup cashews

1 cup freshly squeezed orange juice

1 tablespoon olive oil

1 cup chopped onion

2 tablespoons minced garlic

2 tablespoons minced gingerroot

3 cups peeled and chopped
Garnet yams (about 3 to
4 medium-size yams)

2 quarts vegetable stock

1 (14-ounce) can whole coconut
milk or the water and meat
from a fresh coconut

1 teaspoon orange zest

½ teaspoon sea salt

Freshly ground white pepper,
to taste

⅓ cup chopped cilantro

⅓ cup thinly sliced green onions

This ginger- and citrus-flavored yam soup is a good way to warm a body from the inside out on a cold winter day. Yams are a nutritional winner, loaded with fiber, iron, beta-carotene, and vitamins A and C. The Garnet yam is the queen of them all for flavor and creamy texture, but any variety of yam, sweet potato, or winter squash will work in this recipe. For a simple, tasty, and nourishing meal, serve this soup along with a Spinach, Fennel, and Tangerine Salad (page 81), warm bread, and fresh goat cheese.

Place cashews in a small bowl and pour in the orange juice; cover and set aside to soak for at least 1 hour. You can soak the cashews up to 4 hours—the longer they soak, the creamier they become.

In a heavy-bottom soup pot, heat the oil and sauté the onion for 5 minutes, or until translucent, and then add garlic, gingerroot, yams, and stock and simmer for 8–10 minutes, or until yams are tender.

Place the cashews and orange juice in a blender, blend on high speed until smooth, and set aside. Carefully ladle the soup into the blender, doing this step in two batches for safe handling, cover tightly, and blend on high until smooth and creamy. Return the blended soup to the pot; add the cashew mixture, coconut milk, orange zest, and salt and gently heat, stirring often to prevent scorching. Add additional stock or water as needed to adjust the consistency and season with salt and freshly ground white pepper to taste. Ladle into serving bowls and garnish with cilantro and green onions.

Sun-Dried Tomato Sauce

MAKES 2 CUPS

....

1 cup sun-dried or
   dehydrated tomatoes

2$\frac{1}{2}$ cups hot water or
   vegetable stock

1 cup chopped onion

1 tablespoon extra virgin olive oil

1 tablespoon minced garlic

1 teaspoon sea salt

1 tablespoon agave nectar or
   sweetener of choice, optional

Freshly ground pepper, to taste

1 tablespoon chopped fresh
   oregano or 1 teaspoon dried

1 tablespoon chopped fresh
   basil or 1 teaspoon dried

1 tablespoon chopped fresh parsley

My favorite way to preserve an abundant summer harvest of tomatoes is to slice and sun dry or dehydrate them for use in the cold winter months. This recipe is a wonderful alternative to canned tomatoes and bottled spaghetti sauce. It only takes a few minutes to make once the tomatoes are soaked and soft. Perfect for pizza, or as a topping on your favorite pasta, this simple sauce has a fresh tomato flavor that can only come from rehydrated fresh tomatoes that have not been cooked and canned.

Soak the tomatoes in a bowl with the hot water for 10–15 minutes.

In a heavy-bottom soup pot, heat the oil and sauté the onion for 5 minutes, or until translucent. Place onion, tomatoes, and water into a blender jar. Add the garlic, salt, and agave to the blender and blend until smooth, adding a little more water, if needed, in 1 tablespoon increments to make a saucy consistency.

Tomatoes can vary considerably in texture, sweetness, and flavor. Adjust the seasoning as needed with a little more agave nectar or sweetener of choice and add freshly ground pepper to taste. The sauce is ready to use at this point, or it can be poured into in a heavy-bottom pot or skillet and simmered for 15–20 minutes to develop and deepen the flavor. Stir in the fresh oregano, basil, and parsley before serving.

Red Chile Sauce

6 to 8 large dried mild red chiles, stemmed and seeded

4 cups hot water

2 tablespoons coconut oil

$1^1/_2$ cups coarsely chopped onion

$^1/_2$ cup fresh poblano or pasilla chile pepper, seeded and coarsely chopped

$^1/_2$ cup seeded and coarsely chopped red bell pepper

1 tablespoon minced garlic

$1^1/_2$ teaspoons sea salt

1 tablespoon honey

1 teaspoon Bragg's liquid aminos, optional

2 teaspoons cumin seeds, toasted and ground

Dash of ground cloves

1 tablespoon chopped fresh oregano or $1^1/_2$ teaspoons dried

1 tablespoon chopped fresh epazote or 1 teaspoon dried, optional

1 to 2 tablespoons corn flour or masa harina, to thicken if needed

Traditional marketplaces around the world have beautiful displays of dried peppers that inspire cooks every day. Sauces come to life with the rich and spicy flavors that are found in a wide variety of chiles, ranging from mild to very hot. This recipe is made with mild chiles and a blend of fresh vegetables, but can be spiced up with hot chiles to suit your taste. This may look like a complicated recipe, but it comes together very quickly and makes a versatile sauce that is perfect for enchiladas and can be incorporated into your favorite Mexican dishes.

Over medium-high heat in a dry skillet, toast the red chiles until fragrant, about 1–2 minutes. You can skip this step if you like, but the flavor is best if you take the time to toast the chiles first. Place them in a bowl, cover with the hot water, and soak for 20–30 minutes, or until soft.

In a large skillet over medium heat, add the coconut oil and onion and sauté until translucent, about 6–8 minutes. Add the peppers and continue cooking another 4–5 minutes, or until tender. Stir in the garlic, salt, honey, and aminos.

Drain the rehydrated chiles and reserve the water. If needed, add enough plain water to the chile-soaked water to equal 4 cups. Place the chiles, onions, and peppers into the blender, add the remaining ingredients along with the water, and blend until smooth. Adjust the consistency with a little more water or masa, if needed, to make the sauce thick enough to cling to the tortillas. This sauce freezes well for several months and will last about a week stored in the refrigerator.

Dried Mild Chile Choices
- Ancho or Pasilla: a dried poblano chile
- California red: a dried Anaheim chile
- New Mexico red: similar to the California chile, but hotter

Roasted Tomatillo Sauce

MAKES 3–4 CUPS

2 pounds fresh tomatillos, peeled

1 whole bulb garlic

1 large yellow onion, unpeeled and cut in half

1 large poblano chile pepper

2 jalapeño peppers

1 serrano pepper, optional

1 teaspoon sea salt

1/2 teaspoon cumin, toasted and ground

1/2 cup chopped fresh cilantro

Salsa verde is a classic Mexican sauce made with fresh tomatillo, a tart tomato-like fruit, and mild or hot chiles. This delicious green sauce can be integrated into numerous ethnic dishes and is also tasty as a dip with corn chips or freshly cut veggies. I like to use it for making enchiladas, either alone or in combination with Red Chile Sauce (page 59) for a colorful presentation. For a satisfying south-of-the-border meal, smother a Black Bean Burrito (page 106) with this sauce, top with a sprinkle of cheese, and serve with a scoop of Chunky Guacamole Salad (page 80) on the side.

Preheat oven to 450 degrees F.

For easy removal of the paper-like covering on the tomatillos, soak them in a bowl of water for several minutes before peeling.

Put the whole peeled tomatillos, garlic bulb, onion and peppers on a parchment lined baking sheet, with the onion placed cut side down, and bake for 30–40 minutes, or until soft and beginning to brown. Depending on the size of the peppers, you may need to take the smaller ones out of the oven before the tomatillos and onions are done. Cool peppers enough to handle and remove the stems and seeds. Squeeze the roasted garlic from the papery covering and peel the onion. Carefully place all of the ingredients, except the cilantro, in a blender with a tight-fitting lid, or a food processor, and blend until smooth. Stir in the cilantro and adjust the seasoning with a little more sea salt, if needed.

Pineapple Teriyaki Sauce

MAKES 1 QUART

1 cup nama shoyu, tamari,
   or soy sauce

1 cup mirin or dry sherry

2 cups (1-inch pieces)
   chopped fresh pineapple

1 cup chopped apple

1 cup freshly squeezed orange juice

2 tablespoons molasses

2 tablespoons minced garlic

2 tablespoons minced gingerroot

$1/3$ to $1/2$ cup agave nectar
   or other sweetener, more
   or less depending on the
   sweetness of the pineapple

Teriyaki sauce made with fresh pineapple is in a whole different class than the bottled versions. This simple sauce is a heavenly blend of salt, sweet, and spice and a perfect seasoning for vegetables, tempeh, tofu, meat, fish, or fowl.

Combine all the ingredients in a large saucepan and bring to a boil. Lower the heat, cover, and simmer for 20–30 minutes. Remove the sauce from the heat and carefully pour it into the blender. Cover tightly and blend on high for 1 minute, or until it becomes a slurry. Pour the blended sauce through a steel mesh strainer secured above the empty saucepan to catch the drips. Use the back of a wooden spoon to press the fruit pulp through the strainer, leaving the fibrous pieces behind. Stir the sauce and store in an airtight container in the refrigerator for 5–7 days.

Gado-Gado

MAKES 3 CUPS

1/4 cup minced shallots

1 tablespoon minced garlic

1 tablespoon coconut oil

1 (14-ounce) can coconut milk

1 cup unsalted creamy peanut butter

1 tablespoon minced ginger

2 tablespoons tamari

1 tablespoon agave nectar or honey

2 tablespoons lemon juice
    or rice vinegar

1/2 teaspoon sea salt

1/2 cup vegetable stock or water

Pinch or two of cayenne

1/3 cup chopped cilantro

Gado-Gado is a traditional Indonesian peanut sauce that perfectly complements grilled meats and seafood, tempeh, tofu, steamed vegetables, and fluffy jasmine rice. This is one of those sauces that "blooms" with age and is even better when made the day before you plan to serve it. With the addition of a little rice wine vinegar, Gado-Gado becomes a wonderful dressing for pasta, grain, and chopped veggie salads, or as a dip for Asian Salad Rolls (page 85) or Veggie Sushi Rolls (page 102).

Sauté the shallots and garlic in the coconut oil until translucent and put into a blender jar. Add the coconut milk, peanut butter, ginger, tamari, agave nectar, lemon juice, salt, and vegetable stock, and blend until smooth and creamy. Pour the sauce into a double boiler, or place in a stainless steel bowl suspended over a pot of simmering water, for 20–30 minutes to deepen the flavor, stirring often to keep from scorching. Remove from heat and stir in the cayenne and cilantro.

Fresh Mint and Raisin Sauce

MAKES 1 1/2 CUPS

1/2 cup sucanat

1 tablespoon apple cider vinegar

1 cup raisins

1/4 teaspoon lemon zest

2 tablespoons lemon juice

1 cup water

1/2 cup chopped fresh mint

This very tasty sauce is quick and easy to prepare, adding a refreshing sweet accent to grilled lamb, ham, or tempeh burgers. The bright flavor of fresh mint is a wonderful way to balance a heavy meal, and this sauce is a good alternative to the sugary mint sauces of my childhood that were made with prepared jelly. Fresh mint is also a digestive aid, excellent breath freshener, and a tasty embellishment that is always appreciated when offered with a beautiful meal made with love.

In a small saucepan over medium heat, combine all of the ingredients, except the mint. Simmer for 15–20 minutes and cool. Place into a blender or food processor, add the mint, and pulse into a chunky texture or purée into a smooth sauce. Store in an airtight container in the refrigerator for 7–10 days.

Chanterelle Gravy

MAKES 2 CUPS

....

2 tablespoons olive oil

3 tablespoons Ghee (page 150), divided

4 tablespoons unbleached white flour

1$\frac{1}{2}$ cups roasted or regular Fresh Vegetable Stock (page 51)

2 tablespoons minced shallots

1 cup finely chopped chanterelle mushrooms

$\frac{1}{2}$ teaspoon sea salt

$\frac{1}{2}$ cup dry white wine

Pepper, to taste

The chanterelle is a popular wild mushroom that can be found in many parts of the world and is easy to identify with a good field guide and a little experience. Fortunately they can also be found in specialty produce sections of the grocery stores throughout the harvest season, and like all mushrooms, chanterelles can also be dried for use year-round. These precious wild fungi have a distinctive flavor only found in things that grow all on their own in the forest, adding a festive note to any meal. If you can't find fresh chanterelles for this recipe, substitute your favorite wild or cultivated variety of mushroom and enjoy this rich and delicious gravy on meat, potatoes, grains or other savory dishes.

In a large skillet over medium-high heat, heat the oil, 2 tablespoons Ghee, and the flour, stirring often with a wooden spoon or whisk until it begins to bubble, smells nutty, and turns a golden brown. Slowly dribble hot stock into the roux, stirring constantly until all of the liquid is smoothly incorporated. Lower the heat and simmer for 10–15 minutes, or longer, stirring often, until it looks silky and the floury flavor is gone.

While the gravy is simmering, place the remaining Ghee in a separate skillet, add the shallots and cook for 1 minute, stirring constantly. Add the chanterelles and salt and continue cooking until the mushrooms have expressed their liquid. When the juices begin to evaporate, pour in the wine to deglaze the bottom of the pan. Add the mushroom mixture to the simmering gravy and adjust the thickness with a little more stock, if needed. Simmer for another 10 minutes to marry the flavors and season to taste with salt and pepper. I like to serve this smooth gravy with bite-size pieces of chantrelles, but for those who don't like the texture of mushrooms but love the flavor, pour the gravy and mushrooms into a blender and blend on high speed until smooth.

Tahini-Miso Gravy

MAKES 3 CUPS

3 tablespoons unrefined sesame oil

2 tablespoons minced shallot

1 teaspoon minced garlic

3 tablespoons whole wheat pastry or unbleached white flour

$^1\!/_2$ cup raw tahini (see glossary)

2 cups Fresh Vegetable Stock (page 51) or water

$^1\!/_3$ cup white or red miso (see glossary)

This flavorful and nutritious gravy is good on just about anything, and is a perfect topping for baked tempeh, chicken, meat, tofu, cooked grains, steamed vegetables or mashed potatoes. Tahini is a ground sesame paste, or seed butter, and an excellent source of calcium and vitamin C.

Heat the oil in a medium-size saucepan, add the shallot and garlic and sauté on medium-low heat for 2–3 minutes, or until translucent. Add the flour and cook, stirring constantly, until the flour is lightly browned and has a nutty aroma. Remove the pan from the heat, stir in the tahini, adding a little stock while you briskly whisk to form a paste.

Return the pan to the heat and slowly add the remaining stock, stirring constantly to keep from scorching. Continue to cook until the gravy consistency is to your liking, adding a little more stock if too thick. Remove the pan from the heat, add the miso, and stir or whisk to blend evenly. Serve hot and store in an airtight jar in the refrigerator for 5–7 days.

Fresh raw tahini can be made at home, with a Vita-Mix (see glossary) or a high-speed blender or food processor. For toasted tahini, place 2 cups of raw sesame seeds on a baking sheet and bake at 350 degrees F for 4–6 minutes, or until golden. Do not over bake or they will become bitter. Cool completely before proceeding. If you are using a Vita-Mix, place 2 cups of the raw or toasted sesame seeds in the blender and carefully secure the top. Set it on variable speed, turn it to low, and quickly increase to high. Blend for 1–2 minutes, using the tamper to press the mixture down, until smooth and creamy. If you are using a high-speed blender or food processor, add $^1\!/_3$ to $^1\!/_2$ cup of vegetable oil to the seeds to help it blend. Stop and scrape the sides of the container several times, pushing the seeds into the blades until the mixture is smooth. Tahini can be stored in an airtight jar in the refrigerator for several weeks.

Salads and Salad Dressings

Sprouts

Sprouts are living foods rich in vitamins, minerals, proteins, and enzymes and research encourages us to integrate these tasty baby plants into our diet. Sprouts are very easy to grow yourself, and children especially love to watch the process, and eat these sweet and crunchy super foods by the handful. Look for a variety of viable organic grains, seeds, and nuts to sprout at your local natural food store or from numerous online sources. Soaked and sprouted grains, seeds, and nuts are deeply nourishing foods that can be tossed into salads, kneaded into breads, and added to savory dishes, soups, and smoothies. Amazing, completely raw meals of traditional and ethnic cuisine can be made using sprouts as the foundation. Enjoy these nutritious and delicious little gems as a regular part of a healthy, balanced diet.

SIMPLE SPROUTING INSTRUCTIONS

Seeds will soak up two to three times their volume in water, so choose the container you want to sprout them in accordingly. Sort through the seeds and remove any broken or damaged ones to prevent spoilage. Place the sorted seeds in a one-gallon, half-gallon, or quart jar, depending on the amount of seed and yield, and fill with fresh water. Cover the opening with a piece of cotton cheesecloth or wire mesh screen secured with a rubber band. Drain off the water, refill, and soak the seeds for the allotted time (see chart).

The seeds must be drained and rinsed with fresh water at least twice a day, especially in warm weather. When the proper soaking time has lapsed, drain the water and fill the jar with fresh water. Drain and rinse the seeds a second time. Place the jar in a cool dark place at a 45-degree angle, where it can continue to drain and the opening has good airflow. Alternately, you can use a sprouting bag. Once or twice a day while the seeds are sprouting, fill the jar with fresh water, and gently swish it around so you don't break the little shoots. Drain off the excess water and do it again to keep the sprouts from souring as they grow. Each day thereafter, repeat the process until your sprouts are ready to eat. Store finished sprouts in the refrigerator for 3–5 days. They will continue to grow, but more slowly; so you may need to rinse and drain again, even when stored in the refrigerator, to keep them from spoiling. The seeds listed in the chart will make from 2 cups to 2 quarts of finished sprouts, depending on the variety used.

Sprouting Chart

SEED, NUT, OR BEAN	QUANTITY	HOURS SOAKING	DAYS SPROUTING	CUPS YIELD
Alfalfa	3 tablespoons	6–8	4–5	3–4
Almond	1 cup	8–10	2	4
Amaranth	3 tablespoons	4–6	3	3
Adzuki	½ cup	12	3	4
Barley	1 cup	10	2–3	4
Broccoli	3 tablespoons	6–8	3–4	3
Brown rice	1 cup	8–10	3	1½
Buckwheat	1 cup	8–12	2	2
Chia	1 tablespoon	4–6	2–3	1½
Chive	1 tablespoon	4–6	4–5	1½–2
Clover	1 tablespoon	6–8	3–4	2½
Fenugreek	¼ cup	8–10	3–4	3
Flax	1 tablespoon	6–8	3–4	1
Garbanzo	1 cup	12	2	1½
Kamut	1 cup	8–12	1–3	1½
Lentil	1 cup	8–10	2–4	4
Millet	1 cup	6–8	2	1½
Mung	1 cup	8–10	5	4
Mustard	3 tablespoons	6	4	4
Oat Groat	1 cup	8–10	3	2
Pea	1 cup	10	2	1½
Quinoa	1 cup	4–6	1–3	1½–2
Radish	3 tablespoons	6	3–5	3–4
Rye	1 cup	8–10	3–4	3
Sesame	1 cup	6	1	1½
Spelt	1 cup	6	1–2	3
Sunflower	1 cup	8	2	2
Wheat	1 cup	10–12	2–3	2–3
Wild rice	1 cup	12	3–4	1½–2

The Basic Green Salad
(and more)

Tender greens are the foundation of all great salads, and the ones we choose to use
are dependent on the season, the freshness of what's available, and the whim of
the cook on that particular day. Freshness is a must with all raw salads and inspires
many a gardener to get their hands in the dirt and nurture seeds to grow. Next to
your own garden, the farmers market is by far the best place to purchase fresh
organic greens and other salad vegetables, directly from the farmer at a fair price.
My grandmother used to emphasize the importance of "eating a rainbow of fresh
food" every day for good health, a glowing complexion, and balanced emotions.
Salads were her specialty and every day throughout my childhood I happily ate her
fresh creations because she always made them taste great! Again, it's all about the
freshness of the ingredients, and organic produce usually has the most tender, tasty,
and interesting selections to choose from. Choose an assortment of greens, roots,
flowers, fruits, and other vegetables to get you going. Be playful with your choices,
combine interesting flavors, shapes, textures, and colors, either a few at a time or in
a medley of many, depending on what you're serving.

HOW TO WASH AND STORE SALAD GREENS

When washing greens, begin by filling a large bowl with very cold water, then cut the stem end off of the head of lettuce or greens and carefully separate the leaves. Place them in the water and gently swish around until all the dirt and silt is removed. (Sometimes you'll need to gently rub with your fingers to get it off.) Be sure to thoroughly wash and dry your greens completely so the dressing will cling nicely and won't taste watered down. A good quality salad spinner will serve you well for many years and is worth the investment. If you don't have a spinner, remove the washed greens from the bowl of water and let them drip-dry in a colander or lay the leaves on half of a clean cotton cloth, fold the cloth over the tops, and gently pat dry. If you're not going to be eating your washed and dried greens right away, put them in a reusable green bag (see glossary) and store in the refrigerator. These useful bags will keep most greens fresh for at least 10 to 12 days without wilting, and denser vegetables for 2 to 3 weeks or longer. As an alternative, store your washed greens in an airtight plastic bag or container, with a paper towel or cotton cloth placed in the middle to absorb excess moisture. Store prepared salad greens in the bottom of the refrigerator for up to 1 week.

Greens come in many sizes; a good way to determine the amount needed is to plan between 2 to 4 cups of greens plus $1/4$ to $1/3$ cup assorted vegetables per serving, depending on the variety of greens and other veggies used. Fresh salads are one of the cornerstones of a balanced and healthy diet. Remember when choosing greens that the darker the color of green, the more nutrients and the best value for your food dollar.

STANDARD AND SPECIALTY LETTUCES
- Iceburg lettuce: A compact and crispy lettuce that can be easily held and transported when refrigerated
- Romaine lettuce: Standard and heirloom varieties have a crisp rib running up the center of long deep green or red speckled leaves
- Leaf Lettuce: Large wavy-edged leaves with a slightly crunchy but light quality
- Butter Lettuce: Large ruffled, light green, dark green, or rosy speckled tender leaves
- Commonly Found Heirloom Varieties: Bibb, Red and Green Oak Leaf, and Lollo Rosso
- Cabbage: Green, red, heirloom, and Oriental varieties

BABY GREENS

Great salads are much more than just lettuce, and any tender leafy green that you can harvest while still small in the garden, or buy from your local suppliers, can be eaten raw in a composed salad. Baby greens can be found packaged individually or in specialty mixes at the farmers market or produce section of most supermarkets. Better yet, plant a few of your favorites in the garden, or in pots on the porch, and harvest fresh tender leaves as needed. This will keep your plants producing throughout the growing season and give you fresh accents for your daily salad. Whether you grow your own or buy them, add nourishing baby greens to any tossed green salad for a beautiful and flavorful accent.

- Arugula: An elongated peppery leaf with a tangy finish
- Beet: A hint of sweetness in a tender green
- Belgian Endive: Slightly bitter white and yellow spear-shaped leaves
- Bok Choy: A crunchy and flavorful Asian green
- Chard: A mild-flavored hearty green
- Dandelion: A slightly bitter tasting wild and cultivated green
- Frisee: An endive with fuzzy leaves
- Kale: Slightly sweet and very nutritious
- Mache or Corn Salad: Small round leaves with a light nutty flavor
- Mizuna: A mild-flavored Asian green with jagged edges
- Mustard: Hot and spicy flavor, use sparingly
- Radicchio: A slightly bitter red and white leaf
- Spinach: Mild flavor, use like lettuce
- Tatsoi: A mildly spicy Asian green
- Watercress: A slightly peppery wild and cultivated green

LEAFY HERBAL ACCENTS

- Basil: Anise-like flavored leaves and comes in many different varieties
- Chives: Mild onion-flavored shoots and flowers
- Cilantro: The leaves of the young coriander plant
- Dill Weed: Aromatic and refreshing
- Fennel: Licorice or anise flavor
- Mint: Spicy tang
- Parsley: Italian and curly varieties
- Savory: Bold spicy flavor
- Sorrel: Strong lemony flavor, use sparingly
- Tarragon: Strong anise-like flavor
- Thyme: Piquant and lemony flavor

ROOTS AND FIRM VEGGIES FOR SALADS

Dense vegetables can be sliced, diced, grated, or cut into matchstick pieces and tossed with greens in a composed salad or artfully arranged on the top in a pretty mandala pattern depending on your mood and the time you want to put into making the salad. Try new ingredients and keep changing what you put into your salads as the seasons come and go. Play with different treatments of dense vegetables; for example, baby veggies can be left whole and the larger more mature ones can be grated, julienned, or cut into matchstick pieces to balance their weight with the more delicate greens. Tomatoes and

avocados, fruits that are often classified as vegetables, are standard fare for salad lovers and garnish salads beautifully. Other fruits like fresh berries, citrus, mango, papaya, kiwi, and pomegranate seeds can also dress up your salad creations with flavor, color, and pizzazz. Use about $1/4$ to $1/3$ cup per serving.

- Beet: Sliced thinly, matchstick cut, grated, or whole
- Broccoli: Broken into small florets or chopped
- Cabbage: Very thinly sliced green or purple
- Carrots: Sliced thinly, matchstick cut, grated, or whole baby
- Cauliflower: Broken into small florets or chopped
- Celery: Sliced or tender whole ribs
- Corn: Kernels cut from the cob

- Cucumbers: Chopped or sliced into rounds or spears
- Fennel: Thinly sliced or chopped
- Jicama: Sliced, chopped, or grated
- Kohlrabi: Sliced, chopped, or grated
- Onions (red, green, and white): Sliced, diced, or whole baby
- Peas: Shelled and whole
- Radishes: Sliced, grated, or whole baby

EDIBLE FLOWERS

Flowers have embellished our food with flavor and color ever since the first caveman, or more likely woman, came home with a supper foraged from the wilderness. These days, edible flowers are most often used for decoration. Fresh colorful petals are found beautifully arranged around the layers of wedding cakes, adorning tropical entrées in fancy restaurants, and sprinkled on the fresh garden salads of kitchens that are lucky enough to have them growing nearby. The flowers from any culinary and most medicinal herbs growing in your garden, or in the wild, can be used as a flavor accent in seasonal recipes or as a naturally beautiful garnish. This list is a sample of the most commonly used edible flowers. To be safe, I recommend using a garden or field guide until you can confidently identify the edible flowers from the non-edible varieties.

- Angelica: White and yellow flowers with a mild celery flavor
- Borage: Star-shaped blue flower with a slight cucumber flavor
- Calendula Petals: Yellow and orange hued petals that have a saffron-like spicy flavor
- Carnation: Spicy clove-like flavor
- Chive: Bright bluish-purple flowers with a mild onion flavor
- Gardenia: Light sweet flavor
- Honeysuckle: Syrupy sweet nectar
- Impatiens: Not much flavor, but pretty
- Lavender: Use this fragrant culinary French herb sparingly in food and generously for pretty presentations
- Lilac: Pungent lemony taste
- Nasturtium: Yellow to orange hued flower with a pungent peppery flavor
- Pansy or Violet: Mild sweet-tart flavor
- Rose: Sweet and aromatic flavor
- Sage Blossoms: Musty strong flavor, use sparingly
- Scented Geranium: Multi-flavored depending on plant (rose, lemon, mint, and others)
- Squash Blossoms: Subtle squash flavor, used for garnishing, or can be stuffed and baked
- Yucca: The petals have sweet nectar and are the only edible part of this wild plant

Coleslaws and Cabbage Salads

Raw cabbage is the foundation of coleslaw and has been a staple ingredient of indigenous diets throughout the world. It is a versatile plant that can be eaten raw, cooked, or fermented. Cabbage is packed with essential nutrients like vitamin C and vitamin K, as well as numerous antioxidants, and is also a good source of fiber. Coleslaws can be made in many different ways depending on the variety of cabbage, the other ingredients, and the kind of dressing you choose to season it with. For the best flavor and texture, look for firm dense heads of cabbage with leaves that look shiny and feel crisp. When I make coleslaw, I like to slice the cabbage very thinly by hand, or with a food processor when I'm cooking for a crowd, but some folks prefer to grate it, making the pieces even smaller. Either way will work fine for the following recipes. Cabbage is a nutrition-packed fresh whole food that can be easily grown, or cheaply purchased, providing us with fresh salads all throughout the year.

Simple Fall Slaw

SALAD

2 cups thinly sliced or
grated green cabbage

²/₃ cup grated carrot

²/₃ cup diced celery

¼ cup thinly sliced green onions

¼ cup chopped fresh dill

¼ cup chopped fresh parsley

DRESSING

3 tablespoons apple cider vinegar

2 to 3 tablespoons agave nectar
or sweetener of choice

½ teaspoon dry mustard

2 tablespoons extra virgin olive oil

¼ teaspoon sea salt

Freshly ground pepper, to taste

In a large glass or stainless steel mixing bowl, toss the cabbage, carrot, celery, green onions, dill, and parsley to combine.

In a separate bowl, whisk together the vinegar, agave nectar, mustard, oil, salt, and pepper; toss with the prepared vegetables. Allow the coleslaw to sit for at least several minutes before serving to let the flavors marry, and eat within an hour of making if you like your veggies crunchy. If you don't mind eating your coleslaw a bit limp, it can be kept for several days in an airtight container in the refrigerator.

South-of-the-Border Slaw with Chile-Lime Dressing

....

CHILE-LIME DRESSING

$^1/_3$ cup plain Yogurt (page 141)

$^1/_4$ sour cream, Mayonnaise (page 139), or Vegenaise

$^1/_4$ teaspoon lime zest

1 tablespoon freshly squeezed lime juice

1 jalapeño, minced

$^1/_2$ teaspoon adobo sauce from canned chipotle peppers, optional

1 to 2 teaspoons minced garlic

$^1/_4$ teaspoon sea salt

SALAD

2 cups thinly sliced or grated green cabbage

$^1/_2$ cup grated carrot

$^1/_2$ cup diced red bell pepper

$^1/_2$ cup diced jicama

$^1/_2$ cup grated red radish

$^1/_3$ cup thinly sliced green onion

$^1/_3$ cup chopped cilantro

Whisk all dressing ingredients together until smooth. Combine all salad ingredients in a large mixing bowl and toss with the Chile-Lime Dressing. Allow the coleslaw to sit for at least several minutes before serving to let the flavors marry, and eat within an hour of making if you like your veggies crunchy. If you don't mind eating your coleslaw a bit limp, it can be kept for several days in an airtight container in the refrigerator.

Asian Cabbage Salad

ASIAN DRESSING

2 tablespoons unrefined sesame oil

1 tablespoon toasted sesame oil

4 tablespoons rice wine vinegar

1 tablespoon minced garlic

2 teaspoons grated ginger

2 tablespoons agave nectar

1 to 2 tablespoons nama shoyu, tamari, or soy sauce

Dash of cayenne

Red chile flakes, optional

SALAD

4 cups finely shredded Chinese cabbage

1 cup diagonal-cut fresh snow peas

$^1/_3$ cup matchstick-cut carrots

$^1/_3$ cup matchstick-cut daikon radish, optional

$^1/_4$ cup very thinly sliced red bell pepper

$^1/_3$ cup diagonally sliced green onion

$^1/_4$ cup chopped cilantro

2 tablespoons chopped mint

$^1/_2$ cup lightly toasted, cooled, and chopped cashews

Whisk all dressing ingredients together until smooth. Combine all salad ingredients in a large mixing bowl and toss with Asian dressing. Allow the coleslaw to sit for at least several minutes before serving to let the flavors marry, and eat within an hour of making if you like your veggies crunchy. If you don't mind eating your coleslaw a bit limp, it can be kept for several days in an airtight container in the refrigerator.

Red Cabbage and Pineapple Salad

MAPLE CREAM DRESSING

1/3 cup plain Yogurt (page 141)

1/3 cup Mayonnaise (page 139)

1/3 cup sour cream or Crème
  Fraîche (page 144)

3 tablespoons maple syrup

1 tablespoon fresh lemon juice

1/2 teaspoon dry mustard

1/4 teaspoon sea salt

SALAD

5 cups red cabbage, quartered
  and very finely sliced or grated

1 cup grated carrot

2 cups (1/2-inch chunks)
  chopped fresh pineapple

1/4 cup finely chopped
  Italian parsley

1/4 cup Tamari-Toasted sunflower
  seeds (page 147)

This sweet and creamy cabbage salad is perfect for encouraging kids to eat a good amount of this nutrient rich purple food. Pineapple is high in the antioxidants vitamin C, vitamin E, beta-carotene, selenium, and other essential nutrients that can help to reduce the risks of numerous chronic diseases, and adds a tropical note to this refreshing salad. The pineapple is sweet and delicious in this salad but can be substituted with chopped apples, firm pears, or raisins and topped with lightly roasted or dehydrated almond, cashew, walnut, or pecan pieces for a seasonal variation.

Combine all dressing ingredients in a small mixing bowl and whisk until smooth.

In a large mixing bowl, combine the cabbage, carrot, pineapple, and parsley. Pour Maple Cream Dressing over the salad and toss to coat evenly. Cover and chill for at least 1 hour before serving to develop the best flavor, and eat within an hour of making if you like your veggies crunchy. If you don't mind eating your coleslaw a bit limp, it can be kept for several days in an airtight container in the refrigerator.

To serve, garnish with the sunflower seeds.

Cucumber, Yogurt, and Mint Salad

MAKES 2 1/2 CUPS

2 cups very thinly sliced cucumber, peeled, if not organic, and seeded, if necessary

1 cup plain Yogurt (page 141)

1 tablespoon fresh lime juice

1/3 cup chopped fresh mint

1/3 cup chopped fresh cilantro, optional

1 teaspoon minced garlic

1/4 teaspoon sea salt

In Greek, Indian, Russian, and Asian cuisine there are numerous recipes for cooling cucumber salads, usually served to balance hot and spicy dishes. The flavor, texture, and water content of cucumbers can vary considerably, depending on the variety and how they were grown. Cucumbers that are shiny, firm, and organically grown usually have the best flavor and are worth seeking out at local farmers market during the warm summer months. If the cucumbers are a bit bitter, soak the slices in cold salted water for 30 minutes to 1 hour, rinse, and drain well before adding them to the other ingredients. Serve this refreshing salad with Company Kitcheri (page 101) and hot Grill Bread (page 163) or Chapatis (page 155).

Combine all the ingredients in a mixing bowl and serve chilled. This dish does not store well; however, leftovers can be kept in an airtight container in the refrigerator for a day or two.

Chunky Guacamole Salad

MAKES 4–6 SERVINGS

2 medium-size ripe avocados

1 to 2 tablespoons fresh lemon
    or lime juice, to taste

$1/2$ cup finely chopped white onion

$1/3$ cup finely chopped
    red bell pepper

$1/3$ cup finely chopped celery

$1/3$ cup finely chopped carrot

$1/3$ cup finely chopped
    jicama, optional

1 tablespoon minced garlic

$1/2$ teaspoon toasted and
    ground cumin

$1/2$ teaspoon sea salt

$1/2$ teaspoon Bragg's liquid
    aminos, optional

1 jalapeño, minced

$1/4$ cup chopped cilantro

$1/2$ cup chopped fresh tomato

The addition of fresh vegetables transforms this traditional avocado dip into a wonderful salad packed with nutrition, enzymes, and south-of-the-border spice. The mellow flavor of white onions is my preference in this recipe, but red, yellow, or green varieties will work equally well. Enjoy this salad as a dip with homemade corn chips or crackers for a perfect light lunch or quick snack. To make Chunky Guacamole Salad into a complete and satisfying meal, toss baby greens with a little Creamy Cilantro Dressing (page 96), top with a big scoop of the Chunky Guacamole Salad and sprinkle with Crispy Tempeh Crumbles (page 146). Serve a basket of warm Corn Tortillas (page 154), corn chips, or crackers on the side.

In a medium-size mixing bowl, mash avocados with the lemon or lime juice, leaving small chunks of avocado intact as you go. Add the remaining ingredients and stir to combine. Serve immediately.

Spinach, Fennel, and Tangerine Salad with Maple Pecans

MAKES 4–6 SERVINGS

....

MAPLE PECANS

1 cup pecan halves and pieces

1/4 cup maple syrup

SALAD

1 pound baby spinach leaves,
   washed and dried

4 medium-size tangerines, peeled,
   sectioned, and cut in half

1 cup trimmed, cored,
   quartered, and very thinly
   sliced fresh fennel bulb

DRESSING

3 tablespoons raw apple
   cider vinegar

1/4 cup extra virgin olive oil

1 tablespoon maple syrup

2 teaspoons Dijon mustard

1 teaspoon minced garlic

1/4 teaspoon sea salt

Freshly ground white pepper,
   to taste

In the cold winter months a green salad of fresh spinach, tender fennel, and sweet tangerines can be made from seasonal offerings. Tangerines, a variety of the Mandarin orange, are high in vitamin C and other essential vitamins and minerals. Fresh fennel bulbs are good for digestion and have a mild anise-like flavor. The sweet crunch of yummy maple pecans makes this salad a family favorite.

Preheat the oven to 300 degrees F.

Toss the pecans and maple syrup in a bowl to coat evenly and then spread out on a parchment-covered baking sheet. Bake the pecans just until they become fragrant, about 8–10 minutes. Because of their high oil content, nuts will continue to cook even after you take them out of the oven, so watch carefully to prevent scorching. Remove from the oven and cool. To keep pecans fresh, store in an airtight jar for up to 1 week.

In a large salad bowl combine the spinach, tangerines, and fennel. Place all the dressing ingredients in a small bowl, whisk to combine, pour over the salad and toss to evenly coat. Garnish with the pecans and serve.

Fennel bulbs, stems, and leaves can be eaten either raw or cooked. If you have a mandolin, by all means use it for slicing, if not, a sharp knife will work fine. This flavorful bulb adds a distinctive note to your favorite pasta sauce and also tastes great in a medley of roasted veggies. Another wonderful way to enjoy fennel and bring out the natural sweetness is to cut the bulb into quarters and grill the wedges on an open fire. Raw or cooked, fennel is a flavorful and versatile winter vegetable that is well worth exploring and integrating into your diet.

Tempeh Salad

....

1 (8-ounce) package multigrain tempeh, cut into $1/4$-inch cubes

1 tablespoon organic vegetable broth powder (see glossary)

$1/4$ teaspoon sea salt

$2/3$ cup Vegenaise or Mayonnaise (page 139)

2 teaspoons stone-ground mustard

1 teaspoon Bragg's liquid aminos

1 tablespoon nutritional yeast

1 teaspoon minced garlic

$1/2$ cup sunflower seeds

$1/3$ cup thinly sliced green onions

$1/2$ cup finely chopped celery

$1/2$ cup diced red bell pepper

$1/3$ cup grated carrot

$1/3$ cup finely chopped fresh parsley

2 tablespoons finely chopped fresh dill or 1 tablespoon dried

Sea salt and freshly ground pepper

Tempeh can be an acquired taste for some folks, and this recipe is a good one for introducing the unique flavor of this Indonesian staple to those who are skeptical of new foods. Lightly steamed and seasoned tempeh adds a nutty foundation of flavor to the crunchy vegetables and creamy dressing in this delicious and high-protein salad. Serve this tasty tempeh salad with sliced tomatoes and fresh sprouts in place of tuna or egg salad in a sandwich, or tuck a spoonful into endive spears for a low carbohydrate version. I like to scoop up this hearty salad with rye crackers as a snack, or wrap it in a sprouted grain tortilla with baby greens for a satisfying high-protein meal that is low on fat and full of flavor.

Place the tempeh in a small saucepan with the vegetable broth powder and sea salt. Add enough water to completely cover the tempeh and simmer over low heat until all the water has evaporated, about 15 minutes. Set aside to cool.

Combine the Vegenaise, mustard, aminos, and nutritional yeast in a medium bowl. Add the garlic, sunflower seeds, green onions, celery, bell pepper, carrot, parsley, and dill. Stir to combine. Add the completely cooled tempeh; mix well and season to taste with salt and pepper.

Hummus, Avocado, and Slaw Salad Wrap

MAKES 4 WRAPS

WRAP SLAW

2 cups shredded romaine or
   other firm dark green lettuce

²/₃ cup shredded cabbage, any color

1 cup grated carrot

¹/₂ cup chopped green onion

¹/₃ cup grated red radish

¹/₄ cup chopped Italian parsley

4 each extra large Whole
   Grain Tortillas (page 155)
   or big wraps of choice

2 cups Hummus (page 132)

1 ripe avocado, quartered and sliced

1 cup chopped tomato

¹/₂ pound feta cheese, crumbled

1 cup fresh sunflower
   sprouts, optional

1 cup salad dressing of
   choice, optional

Pack a wrap into a cooler with a little container of the dressing on the side and enjoy a fresh, satisfying, and nourishing meal while at work, school, or play.

Toss all slaw ingredients together in a bowl to combine; set aside.

Warm the wraps briefly in a hot skillet to keep from cracking as you roll them up around the filling. Spread the center of each wrap with the hummus, leaving an inch or so margin around the edges. Put 1 cup slaw on the lower half of the hummus. Evenly place the avocado, tomato, cheese, and sprouts, if using, on top of the slaw and drizzle 1 tablespoon of salad dressing evenly over all. Fold the bottom end of the tortilla over the filling, gently squeezing to compress. Carefully fold in the sides and tuck them in as you go, rolling up the tortilla burrito style.

For a pretty presentation, cut the wrap in half on the diagonal and set it on end, with the cut side up. Serve each wrap with a little side of salad dressing for those who like to drizzle more on top as they eat it. Most wraps will last in an airtight container for a day or two in the refrigerator or cooler, but are always best when eaten fresh.

Wraps have become the new fast food and a healthy alternative to burgers and fries for those in need of a quick and nutritious meal. Thanks to the popularity of big tortillas, the world of wraps has grown from the basic burrito into a fabulous way to hold just about anything. Whatever goes into a sandwich or salad can be embellished, seasoned, and wrapped. Salad wraps are a great way to get a big helping of wholesome fresh vegetables in a savory bundle that you can eat with your hands. Add strips of leftover turkey, chicken, meat, or thin slices of cold smoked wild salmon for additional flavor and nutrition. Wraps can be purchased in many varieties, so choose whatever kind you like, but please read the label as many of the commercial brands have artificial flavoring, coloring and other questionable ingredients. If you have the time, fresh wraps can be easily made from organic whole grains at a fraction of the cost of store-bought ones.

Asian Salad Rolls with Chile-Lime Dipping Sauce and Gado-Gado

MAKES 20 ROLLS

....

CHILE-LIME DIPPING SAUCE

1 tablespoon minced garlic

1 teaspoon minced ginger

1 to 3 fresh jalapeños, serranos, or Thai chiles, stemmed, seeded, and minced, or $1/4$ to 1 teaspoon bottled Sambal chile sauce, depending on how hot and spicy you like it

2 tablespoons fish sauce or Bragg's liquid aminos for a vegan version

$1/3$ cup hot water

1 tablespoon fresh lime juice

$1/2$ teaspoon lime zest

$1/4$ cup agave nectar syrup

SALAD ROLLS

20 (12-inch rounds) sheets rice paper wrappers (see glossary)

2 to 3 medium-size heads of very fresh tender lettuce, washed, drained, and dried well

1 cup fresh mung bean sprouts, or your favorite variety

1 cup matchstick-cut or coarsely grated carrot

$1/2$ cup grated radishes

2 cups cilantro leaves, large and tough stems removed

1 cup fresh mint leaves, stems removed

1 cup basil leaves, stems removed

Gado-Gado (page 62)

Salad rolls are one of my favorite meals and a refreshing way to enjoy the abundance of greens that a summer garden offers. Rice papers can be tricky to handle, so take your time, follow the directions below, and with a bit of practice you'll be rolling like the pros. Make sure to have all of your ingredients prepared and set on the table in an assembly line in the order you plan to use them. This recipe may look complicated, but once you get the hang of it and see how easy it is to make these delicious rolls, you'll be enjoying them often. Asian salad rolls travel well for a few hours in a cooler and are always a big hit and a welcome change in lunch boxes and on potluck tables that usually have the same old fare.

Whisk all sauce ingredients together in a bowl; set aside.

Prepare rice paper wrappers by filling a large shallow bowl with hot water, about 120 degrees F. Keep a kettle of hot water near by and add a little at a time to maintain the water temperature while you roll. Dip one rice paper at a time into the water to soften, count to ten, remove and drain briefly over the bowl before setting on a flat surface. Place a leaf or two of lettuce and a sprinkling of bean sprouts, carrot, and radishes on the bottom half of the wrapper, leaving a 1-inch margin around the edges. Lay several cilantro, mint, and basil leaves across the top of the veggies, making sure you arrange the ingredients evenly to allow for easy rolling.

To begin rolling, gently press down on the ingredients to make them compact, and fold both sides of the rice paper towards the center. Next, take the bottom part of the round, fold it over the compressed ingredients and carefully roll as tightly as possible, without tearing the rice paper, burrito style. It will seem awkward at first, but when you get the hang of it, the assembly will go quickly. The finished salad roll should be tightly rolled, about. $1^1/2$–2 inches in diameter and about 5 inches long. Cut the rolls in half and serve with the dipping sauce and/ or Gado-Gado on the side. For parties, place a bowl of dipping sauce in the center of a large platter and arrange the rolls cut side up in an attractive circular pattern. These salad rolls will hold for a few hours in a cooler with a slightly damp towel laid over them, but are best eaten as soon as possible after they are made.

Kale and Sea Vegetable Salad with Sesame Citrus Dressing

MAKES 4–6 SERVINGS

SESAME CITRUS DRESSING

2 tablespoons rice wine vinegar

$1/2$ cup freshly squeezed orange or tangerine juice

2 tablespoons freshly squeezed lemon juice

2 tablespoons tamari

2 tablespoons raw tahini

2 teaspoons fresh grated gingerroot

1 tablespoon nutritional yeast

1 tablespoon agave nectar or maple syrup

$1/4$ cup unrefined sesame or flax seed oil

SALAD

4 cups very fresh organic kale, stemmed and thinly sliced

$1^1/2$ ($1/2$-inch pieces) cups fresh or rehydrated dried seaweed, Hijiki, Wakame, or sea palm

$1/2$ cup julienned or grated carrots

$1/3$ cup thinly sliced red onion

2 tablespoons raw or lightly toasted sesame seeds

Kale is truly a nutritional gold mine and one of the most flavorful good-for-you greens. Just a plant or two in the garden, or a planter will provide you with a good supply of this fantastic super food. Farmers markets have amazing kale, as well as chard, collards, mustard, and other leafy greens. High in calcium, iron, and many other vital nutrients, fresh leafy green vegetables are essential for good health, and eating them raw is the best way for our body to assimilate the nutrients.

For generations, traditional cultures living by the sea have incorporated sea vegetables into their diets; providing them with vital minerals, vitamins, and protein. But if you don't live near the sea, or prefer to buy seaweed already harvested and dried, a wide variety of sea vegetables can be found in natural food stores, Oriental markets, or from one of many sources online. Try substituting different seaweeds, vegetables, and seasonings to harmonize with the natural seasonal offerings and enjoy the healthy glow that comes with eating nourishing sea vegetables and nutrient-dense dark leafy greens.

In a small bowl, whisk together all of the dressing ingredients until well blended.

Combine the kale, seaweed, carrots, and onion in a large mixing bowl. Add the dressing and then toss, massaging the veggies with your hands to coat evenly while gently squeezing as you go to break down the fiber and soften the greens. Let the salad sit at room temperature for 30 minutes or longer to develop the flavor and allow the vinegar and citrus to "cook" the kale. Garnish each serving with a sprinkling of sesame seeds.

NOTE: *To rehydrate dried seaweed, place it in a bowl, cover with water, and allow to soak for 30–60 minutes, depending on the thickness and kind of seaweed used. Do not throw this mineral rich water away. The leftover water can be gently heated and combined with miso for hot mineral rich beverage, or if you really like the flavor of sea vegetables, add up to $1/2$ cup of the soaking water to the kale and seaweed salad dressing.*

Jewel Salad

JEWEL SALAD DRESSING

6 tablespoons freshly
   squeezed orange juice

2 tablespoons rice vinegar

1 tablespoon honey or agave nectar

$1/3$ cup chopped fresh mint leaves

SALAD

$1/2$ cup minced carrot

$1/2$ cup ($1/4$-inch pieces)
   chopped celery

1 cup ($1/4$-inch pieces)
   chopped pears

1 cup ($1/4$-inch pieces)
   chopped crisp red apple

1 cup ($1/4$-inch pieces)
   chopped green apple

$1/2$ cup ($1/4$-inch pieces)
   chopped Fuyu persimmons

1 cup pomegranate seeds

Jewel salad is a sensual culinary experience. In this seasonal recipe, fall fruits and vegetables are finely chopped for an explosion of flavors that are sure to delight all fresh salad lovers. The fresh fruits, vegetables, and mint add beneficial enzymes to help us to digest the array. Cranberry sauce or Cranberry-Tangerine Relish (page 138) is nicely complemented by the crunchy texture and combination of flavors in this salad, making it a wonderful addition to any Thanksgiving table. The key is to mince and finely chop all of the ingredients carefully into very small jewel-size pieces.

Mix dressing ingredients together and set aside.

Mix salad ingredients in a bowl and toss with dressing. Let it sit at room temperature for at least 1 hour to marry flavors before serving. This salad is best eaten fresh; however, it can be stored in an airtight jar in the refrigerator for 1–2 days but won't be as crunchy.

Salad Dressings

Big garden salads are daily fare in our home, and making a variety of fresh flavorful dressings ensures that everyone will happily eat all their veggies. Tasty salad dressings are very quick and easy to make and are the best way to dress a fresh garden salad. Bottled dressings are full of stabilizers, preservatives, artificial flavors (even natural flavors can contain MSG) and other questionable ingredients. The natural brands can be very expensive, are usually made with low-quality oils, and are often not very tasty. Full-flavored vinegar is well worth the price and will make the very best salad dressings. I always use the highest quality oils and vinegars for my salad dressings because they tend to have considerably more flavor than the cheaper brands, and a little goes a long way. Balancing the tart, sweet, salty, and bitter flavors of the ingredients you use is the secret to making great tasting salad dressings, and this skill can be mastered with practice. The fabulous flavor of freshly made dressings will adorn your beautiful salads in the style they deserve, at a fraction of the cost, and a bowl, whisk, knife, and cutting board are all you need. When making salad dressings, I use a small stainless steel bowl and a little wire whisk, one of the most useful and often used tools in my kitchen. If you like, all of these recipes can be made in just a few moments with a blender, or small food processor, and can be multiplied to make whatever amount you need. I prefer salad dressing made fresh for each meal, but all of the following recipes will store well in an airtight jar in the refrigerator for several days.

Basic Lemon and Olive Oil

MAKES ²/₃ CUP

¼ cup freshly squeezed lemon juice

¼ teaspoon lemon zest

1 tablespoon agave nectar,
    honey, or other sweetener

¼ teaspoon sea salt

¼ teaspoon dry mustard, optional

2 teaspoons minced garlic

1 tablespoon minced shallots

1 tablespoon nutritional
    yeast, optional

Freshly ground pepper, to taste

¹/₂ cup extra virgin olive oil

In a small mixing bowl, briskly whisk all of the ingredients, except the oil, to combine. Continue whisking while drizzling oil into the bowl, 1 tablespoon at a time to emulsify the ingredients and thicken the dressing. Adjust seasoning with additional salt and pepper to taste.

Roquefort Vinaigrette

MAKES 1¹/₃ CUPS

¼ cup freshly squeezed lemon juice

2 teaspoons Dijon mustard

1 teaspoon natural
    Worcestershire sauce

1 teaspoon minced garlic

1 tablespoon minced shallots

2 teaspoons nutritional yeast

Sea salt, optional

Freshly ground pepper, to taste

¹/₂ cup extra virgin olive oil

1 tablespoon finely chopped
    Italian parsley

1 tablespoon finely chopped
    fresh dill or 1 teaspoon dried

¹/₃ cup crumbled Roquefort cheese

In a small straight-side mixing bowl, briskly whisk all of the ingredients, except the oil, herbs, and Roquefort, to combine. Continue whisking while drizzling oil into the bowl, 1 tablespoon at a time to help emulsify the ingredients and thicken the dressing. Add the herbs and Roquefort and mix well. Adjust the seasoning with a little more salt and pepper to taste.

Fresh Herb Vinaigrette

MAKES ABOUT ³/₄ CUP

¹/₃ cup raw apple cider vinegar

2 teaspoons agave nectar, honey, or sweetener of choice

¹/₂ teaspoon Dijon mustard

2 teaspoons minced garlic

1 tablespoon minced shallots, optional

¹/₄ teaspoon sea salt

1 tablespoon nutritional yeast

Freshly ground pepper, to taste

¹/₂ cup extra virgin olive oil

3 tablespoons flax seed oil, optional

3 to 4 tablespoons finely chopped fresh herbs: basil, chives, cilantro, dill, Italian parsley, oregano, tarragon, and thyme—alone or in combination

In a small straight-side mixing bowl, briskly whisk all of the ingredients, except the oil and herbs, to combine. Continue whisking while drizzling oil into the bowl, 1 tablespoon at a time to help emulsify the ingredients and thicken the dressing. Stir in the herbs and adjust seasoning with additional salt and pepper to taste.

Balsamic and Fresh Basil Vinaigrette

¹/₄ cup balsamic vinegar

1 tablespoon minced shallots

1 tablespoon minced garlic

1 tablespoon Dijon mustard

1 tablespoon agave nectar, honey,
   or sweetener of choice

1 tablespoon tamari

Sea salt and freshly ground
   pepper, to taste

¹/₂ cup extra virgin olive oil

2 tablespoons finely
   chopped fresh basil

In a small straight-side mixing bowl, briskly whisk all of the ingredients, except the oil and basil, to combine. Continue whisking while drizzling oil into the bowl, 1 tablespoon at a time to help emulsify the ingredients and thicken the dressing. Stir in the basil and adjust seasoning with more salt and pepper to taste.

Kiwi Vinaigrette

2 kiwi fruits, peeled and quartered
   (about ¹/₃ cup total)

¹/₄ cup rice wine vinegar

¹/₂ teaspoon dry mustard

1 tablespoon chopped red onion

¹/₄ cup extra virgin olive oil

¹/₄ teaspoon sea salt

Freshly ground pepper, to taste

Place all ingredients in a blender and purée on high until smooth.

Dreamy Tahini

MAKES ABOUT ¾ CUP

1 teaspoon minced garlic

¼ cup chopped red onion

¼ cup freshly squeezed lemon juice

1 tablespoon white miso

2 tablespoons tamari

2 tablespoons maple syrup,
   agave nectar, or honey

⅓ cup raw tahini

¼ cup water

¼ cup unrefined sesame or
   extra virgin olive oil

Pinch of cayenne

Place all ingredients in a blender and purée on high until smooth, thinning with water in 1-tablespoon increments as needed.

Rockin' Ranch

MAKES ABOUT 1 1/3 CUPS

1/2 cup buttermilk

1/4 cup Mayonnaise (page 139)

1/4 cup sour cream

1/4 cup plain Yogurt (page 141)

2 tablespoons raw apple
    cider vinegar

1 teaspoon minced garlic

1 tablespoon minced shallots

1/2 teaspoon Dijon mustard

1/2 teaspoon Bragg's liquid aminos

1 tablespoon Spike seasoning

1 tablespoon nutritional yeast

1 tablespoon finely chopped
    Italian parsley

1/4 teaspoon ground celery
    seed, optional

In a small bowl, whisk together all of the ingredients until blended, cover, and refrigerate for at least 20 minutes to marry the flavors.

White Miso, Grapefruit, and Flax seed oil

MAKES 2/3 CUP

3 tablespoons smooth white miso

1/3 cup freshly squeezed
    grapefruit juice

1 teaspoon minced garlic

1/4 cup flax seed oil

1 tablespoon agave nectar

1 tablespoon tamari

In a small bowl, whisk together all of the ingredients until blended, cover, and refrigerate for at least 20 minutes to marry the flavors.

Green Goddess

MAKES ABOUT 1 CUP

¹/₂ cup Mayonnaise (page 139)

¹/₄ cup plain Yogurt (page 141)

¹/₄ cup sour cream

¹/₃ cup chopped Italian parsley, large stems removed

¹/₄ cup thinly sliced green onions or chives

2 tablespoons freshly squeezed lemon juice or rice vinegar

1 teaspoon minced garlic

1 teaspoon finely chopped tarragon, optional

¹/₄ teaspoon sea salt

Freshly ground pepper, to taste

Place all the ingredients in a blender or food processor and purée until smooth.

Chipotle Thousand Island

MAKES 1¹/₂ CUPS

1 cup Mayonnaise (page 139)

¹/₃ cup plain Yogurt (page 141)

1 tablespoon minced garlic

2 tablespoons minced green onions

3 tablespoons minced dill pickle

2 tablespoons minced red pepper

1 teaspoon adobo sauce (from canned chipotle peppers)

In a small bowl, whisk together all of the ingredients until well blended, cover, and refrigerate for at least 20 minutes to marry the flavors.

Creamy Cilantro Dressing

MAKES 1¹/₃ CUPS

....

¹/₃ cup Mayonnaise (page 139)

¹/₄ cup plain Yogurt (page 141)

¹/₄ cup sour cream

1 tablespoon freshly
squeezed lime juice

1 tablespoon freshly squeezed
lemon juice or rice wine vinegar

¹/₄ teaspoon toasted and ground
cumin seeds, optional

¹/₄ teaspoon sea salt

1 tablespoon nutritional yeast

Freshly ground pepper or
cayenne pepper, to taste

2 cups chopped fresh cilantro, large
stems removed and packed

Place all ingredients in a blender, adding the cilantro last, and blend until smooth. If your blender has trouble incorporating the cilantro, turn it off, press the leaves down towards the bottom of the container and continue processing until smooth.

Vegetarian Entrées

Indonesian Tempeh Sticks with Gado-Gado

MAKES 4 SERVINGS

....

1/2 pound tempeh

MARINADE

1/3 cup tamari, nama shoyu, or soy sauce

2 tablespoons fresh lime juice

2 teaspoons minced garlic

1 tablespoon grated ginger

1 teaspoon unrefined or toasted sesame oil

1/2 teaspoon whole or ground coriander

2 to 3 tablespoons honey or agave nectar

1 teaspoon dry mustard

1/4 teaspoon red chile flakes, optional

1/3 cup vegetable stock or water

2 cups Gado-Gado (page 62)

For family gatherings and summer barbecues, bake tempeh sticks or cutlets ahead of time and remove them from the oven when the marinade is fully absorbed, but before they begin to brown. When you're ready to eat, lightly grill the flavor-infused sticks over the coals for a vegetarian protein offering. Make a big batch! These are very yummy morsels and everyone will want a piece or two—not only your grateful vegetarian guests. This is also an excellent marinade for grilled chicken, shrimp, or other meats— just omit the vegetable stock or water from the recipe.

Cut the tempeh cake into 16 sticks, each one 1 x 2-inches and about 1/2-inch thick. Lay the sticks side-by-side in a 9 x 13-inch glass or ovenproof baking dish. Combine marinade ingredients, except for the vegetable stock, in a small bowl, mix well, and pour over the tempeh, wiggling the dish to evenly coat. Cover and let the tempeh marinade for several hours or overnight in refrigerator, turning the pieces over from time to time.

Preheat oven to 350 degrees F.

Pour the vegetable stock over the tempeh and blend it evenly into the marinade. Put the tempeh in the oven and bake for 30–40 minutes, or until most of the liquid is absorbed and the pieces begin to brown. Serve hot with Gado-Gado on the side. Store cooked and cooled tempeh strips in an airtight container in the refrigerator for 5–7 days.

Tempeh soaks up flavors like a sponge, is easy to work with, and can be integrated into almost any meal as a substitute for fish, poultry, or meat as a vegan protein option. Cultured soybeans, usually combined with grains, land and sea vegetables, and other flavorings are fermented to create a cake that is then cut into strips, cutlets, or sprinkles, depending on what you're making. This easily digested high-quality plant protein is simple to work with and ready to be transformed with your creative touch.

Pescadero Pesto Pasta with Tempeh Crumbles

MAKES 4 SERVINGS

....

1 pound brown rice spaghetti
   or pasta of choice

2 tablespoons olive oil

$1/2$ pound grated fresh Asiago

1 cup Crispy Tempeh
   Crumbles (page 146)

PESCADERO PESTO

2 to 3 cups fresh basil leaves,
   finely chopped or chiffonade

$1/3$ cup extra virgin olive oil

$1/2$ teaspoon sea salt

Freshly ground white
   pepper, to taste

$1/2$ cup finely chopped pecans

1 to 2 tablespoons minced
   garlic, to taste

In the little pueblo of El Pescadero near the tip of the Baja Peninsula, they grow amazing organic vegetables, and basil is their number one crop. Pesto can be made the traditional way with a mortar and pestle, or by simply chopping everything very finely by hand. If you are in a hurry, of course this recipe can be made in a food processor in just a few seconds. However, the texture of each ingredient being finely chopped separately and then combined in a chunky mass of green goodness is what makes this dish extraordinary. Serve with sliced tomatoes and a beautiful seasonal veggie platter with your favorite dips on the side for a wholesome summer meal the whole family will enjoy.

Cook spaghetti according to directions until al dente, or done to your liking. While the pasta is cooking, combine the basil, olive oil, salt, pepper, pecans, and garlic in a mixing bowl and set aside.

When the pasta is done, drain, rinse with hot water and return it to the cooking pot. Add the pesto, half of the cheese, and toss to combine, stirring quickly to retain the heat. Serve on warm plates and top each portion with the remaining cheese and $1/4$ cup Crispy Tempeh Crumbles.

Tempeh and Chard Enchiladas

MAKES 6 SERVINGS

1 (8-ounce) package multigrain tempeh, cut into 1/4-inch pieces

3 tablespoons coconut oil, warmed until it melts, divided

2 teaspoons chili powder or Mexican spice mix

1 teaspoon cumin seeds, toasted and ground

2 teaspoons minced garlic

1/4 teaspoon sea salt

1 1/2 cups chopped white onion

6 cups chopped Swiss chard

3 cups Red Chile Sauce (page 59)

12 whole or sprouted wheat tortillas

2 cups grated manchego or Monterey Jack cheese (about 1/2 pound)

Salsa Fresca (page 135)

When the garden manager at Esalen asked me what I could do with the rows and rows of Swiss chard that needed continuous harvesting, I had an opportunity to work with this wonderful garden green in a variety of new and imaginative ways. In this recipe, whole grain tortillas are wrapped around seasoned chard, onions, tempeh, and cheese and finished with a rich red chile sauce. These hearty and satisfying enchiladas are a perfect vegetarian entrée to serve to friends and family who are skeptical of meals without meat and resist trying different foods, like tempeh. This is a delicious and nutritious dish that everyone will enjoy and appreciate.

Preheat oven to 350 degrees F.

In a small mixing bowl, toss the tempeh with the oil, chili powder, cumin, garlic, and sea salt. Spread the pieces evenly in an ovenproof baking dish and bake, turning the pieces with a spatula several times, for 15–20 minutes or until they are sizzling and just begin to brown. Do not over bake; the oil will continue to cook the tempeh even after you take it out of the oven, so watch carefully.

In a large skillet, sauté the onion in the remaining oil for 2 minutes, add the chard, cover, and cook just until the chard is wilted, but the rib and onions are still al dente. Combine the tempeh with the chard mixture and set aside.

Preheat oven to 400 degrees F.

Place 1/2 cup Red Chile Sauce on the bottom of an 11 x 17-inch ovenproof baking dish. Warm a tortilla briefly on a hot grill to prevent it from cracking and dip in the sauce to lightly coat both sides. Place the saucy tortilla in the baking dish and sprinkle 1/3 cup cheese across the center, or omit the cheese for a vegan version. Spoon approximately 1/3 cup of the tempeh mixture on top of the cheese and carefully roll the tortilla around the filling, placing the flap on the bottom to hold the enchilada in place. Repeat the process with the remaining ingredients, reserving 1/2 cup cheese for the top. Cover the enchiladas with the remaining sauce and sprinkle with the remaining cheese. Bake for 15–20 minutes, or until hot and bubbly. Serve with Salsa Fresca, brown rice, South-of-the-Border Slaw (page 76), and a basket of corn chips for a wholesome and satisfying meal.

Company Kitchari

SPICE MIXTURE

1 teaspoon fennel seeds

1 teaspoon cumin seeds

1 teaspoon coriander seeds

1 teaspoon ground turmeric

1/4 teaspoon ground cardamom

Pinch of cinnamon

1 teaspoon sea salt

1 tablespoon Ghee (page 150)
   or coconut oil

KITCHARI

1 tablespoon Ghee (page 150)
   or coconut oil

1 cup chopped onion

2/3 cup chopped celery

2/3 cup chopped yam

1 cup (1/2-inch pieces)
   Portobello mushroom (about
   1 extra large mushroom)

2 teaspoons minced gingerroot

1 tablespoon minced garlic

1 teaspoon minced jalapeño

2 bay leaves

11/2 cups long-grain brown rice

11/2 cups red lentils, rinsed

5 cups water

Kitchari is a classic Indian comfort food consisting of lentils, rice, and vegetables cooked together in one pot along with a fragrant combination of spices. Nourishing kitchari is prescribed as a medicine in the Ayurvedic tradition for cooling, cleansing, and balancing the digestive system, and is usually made without onions or garlic. This version of Kitchari is embellished with caramelized onions, a touch of garlic, and portobello mushrooms for added flavor, slanting it towards the western palate. This is a unique and easy to prepare one-dish meal that can be made with simple ingredients from the larder, garden, and spice shelf. Serve with Cucumber, Yogurt, and Mint Salad (page 79), steamed spinach or chard, and toasted papadums or hot Chapatis (page 155).

In a dry skillet, toast the fennel, cumin, and coriander seeds until fragrant. Cool and grind the spices and combine with the turmeric, cardamom, cinnamon, and sea salt. Pour the toasted spices back into the skillet, add the Ghee, and lightly sauté for 1–2 minutes to develop the flavor.

In a large heavy-bottom soup pot with a tight-fitting lid, sauté the Ghee and onions over medium-high heat until they just begin to brown. Add the celery and yam and cook for 5–6 minutes, stirring frequently. Add the mushroom, ginger, garlic, jalapeño, and bay leaves and continue to stir while it cooks for another 3–4 minutes. Add the spice mixture to the pot and blend evenly into the vegetables. Stir in the rice and lentils, add the water, cover, and bring to a boil. Lower the heat and simmer for 45 minutes, or until all the water has evaporated and the rice and lentils are tender. Garnish with chopped cilantro and serve with lime wedges on the side, if desired.

Veggie Sushi Rolls with Three Sauces

MAKES 10 ROLLS

QUINOA-MILLET SUSHI BLEND

1 cup quinoa

1 cup millet

4 cups water

$1/2$ teaspoon sea salt

$1/4$ cup rice vinegar

1 tablespoon agave nectar
   or sweetener of choice

SEASONED SHIITAKE MUSHROOMS

1 cup sliced fresh shiitake
   mushrooms or substitute
   rehydrated dried shiitakes

$1/3$ cup mirin

2 tablespoons tamari

1 teaspoon minced garlic

2 tablespoons agave nectar,
   honey, or sugar

TRADITIONAL WASABI SAUCE

1 teaspoon Wasabi powder

Water

$1/3$ cup tamari or soy sauce

Hand-rolled sushi is a quick and easy meal and a perfect bundle of nourishing food for hungry kids on the go. I love the flavor and little crunch of quinoa and millet, but if you prefer, use regular white sushi rice or any other cooked grain in its place. Let your imagination go with the fillings—matchstick-cut vegetables, slices of avocado, all kinds of sprouts, fresh shiitake mushrooms, seasoned tofu slices, tempeh salad, fresh seafood, or your favorite sushi ingredients. Individual hand rolls are shaped like an ice cream cone and a fun food to make and eat. You can also use a bamboo sushi mat to roll your sushi in the traditional cylinder and eat it whole or cut into rounds. Serve sushi rolls with one or more of the sauces, Miso Vegetable Soup (page 54), and a fresh garden salad for a light and nourishing meal that can be made year-round with larder staples and seasonal garden offerings. These savory rolls travel well, are perfect for a quick snack, or a welcome change in a sack lunch, especially with an assortment of tasty dipping sauces.

Wash the quinoa and millet until water runs clear and drain well.

In a 4-quart saucepan with a tight-fitting lid, bring the water to a boil, stir in the quinoa, millet, and salt, lower the heat to a simmer, and steam for 20 minutes, or until all the water is absorbed. Remove from heat and let sit, covered, for 10 minutes to retain the moisture in the grains.

In a small bowl, whisk together the rice vinegar and agave nectar. Spoon the quinoa and millet into a large stainless steel or glass mixing bowl, drizzle with the sweetened vinegar, and toss gently. Spread the mixture up the sides of the bowl, stirring several times to release the heat, until it has cooled completely.

In a 2-quart saucepan, simmer sliced shiitakes, mirin, tamari, garlic, and agave nectar for 8–10 minutes. Drain the liquid off the mushroom slices and cool (and save it for flavoring miso soup, salad dressings, or sauces).

To make the traditional wasabi sauce, place a small amount, 1 to 3 tablespoons to begin, of the wasabi powder in a small mixing bowl and add water in 1-tablespoon increments, stirring briskly until it forms a smooth paste. When you have the amount you want, add the tamari and blend well.

ALMOND WASABI SAUCE

$1/2$ cup creamy almond butter

$1/4$ cup rice wine vinegar

1 tablespoon wasabi powder

2 tablespoons tamari

2 tablespoons flax seed oil

1 tablespoon chopped white onion

1 teaspoon chopped ginger

$1/2$ teaspoon Sambal or your
   favorite hot sauce, optional

$1/4$ cup chopped cilantro

CREAMY SESAME SAUCE

$1/2$ cup Mayonnaise (page 139)
   or Vegenaise

$1/3$ cup Yogurt (page 141)

2 tablespoons tahini

3 tablespoons rice wine vinegar

2 tablespoons agave nectar
   or sweetener of choice

1 tablespoon toasted sesame oil

Pickled ginger, optional

10 sheets toasted nori
   seaweed sheets

1 cup matchstick-cut carrots

1 large cucumber, sliced lengthwise,
   seeded and cut into thin strips

1 ripe avocado, cut into thin slices

2 cups baby spinach leaves

1 cup daikon, sunflower, or
   radish sprouts, optional

1 cup Tamari-Toasted sunflower
   seeds (page 147)

To make the almond wasabi sauce, place all of the ingredients into a bowl and whisk until smooth and creamy, adding water in 1-tablespoon increments as needed for the right consistency.

To make the creamy sesame sauce, whisk all the ingredients together in a small bowl and refrigerate until served.

MAKING HAND ROLLS:

Cut a sheet of toasted nori in half and lay it horizontally, shiny side down, on a clean flat surface. Place $1/3$ cup quinoa blend on the left third of the nori sheet, leaving a $1/2$-inch border around edges. Being mindful of the volume you have to work with, lay a small portion of each of the veggies, including the mushrooms, vertically across the middle of the grains and top with a thin layer of spinach and sprouts, if using, and sprinkle with toasted sunflower seeds. Beginning with the side that has the rice on it, fold the corner nearest you over and start to roll, forming a cone shape. Continue rolling until the nori is completely wrapped around the filling and secure the end flap with a dab of water. Drizzle a small amount of your favorite sauce over the top as you eat and garnish with the ginger.

MAKING TRADITIONAL CYLINDERS FOR BITE-SIZED ROLLS:

On a Japanese bamboo sushi-rolling mat, place 1 sheet of toasted nori, shiny side down and even with the lower edge. Lightly wet your hands, to keep the grains from sticking to them, and cover the nori sheet with $1/4$ inch thickness of the quinoa blend, leaving a $1/2$-inch border around edges. Lay a strip of shiitake, carrot, cucumber, avocado, spinach, and sprouts lengthwise across the center of the rice and sprinkle with toasted sunflower seeds. Hold the line of veggies firmly in place with your fingertips and using your thumbs, turn the sushi mat edge nearest you over the filling and give a gentle squeeze. Continue pressing forward to shape into a cylinder, keeping the mat free as you go. Dampen the top edge with a little water and give it another little squeeze to seal. With a sharp knife, slice into 6–8 bite-size pieces, wiping the knife with a wet cloth between cuts. Arrange on a platter, garnish with pickled ginger, and serve the sushi dipping sauces in bowls on the side.

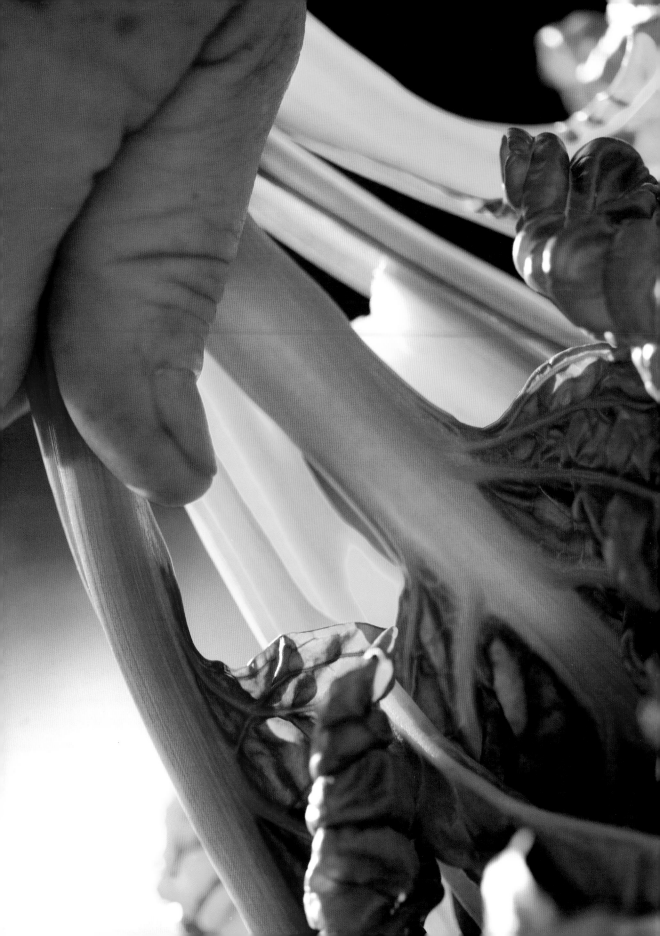

Chard Pie

8 cups thinly chopped or
ribboned chard

1/2 cup thinly sliced green onions

1/3 cup whole wheat pastry
or corn flour

3 eggs or substitute 3/4 cup well
mashed tofu for a vegan version

2 tablespoons nutritional yeast

2 tablespoons minced shallots

1 tablespoon minced garlic

1/2 teaspoon sea salt

Freshly ground pepper, to taste

2 tablespoons olive oil, divided

2 tablespoons Ghee (page 150)
or vegetable oil, divided

Most pies are baked in an oven, but this recipe is quickly prepared on the stove top, making it a perfect dish for camping trips and traveling kitchens. Top with a dollop of horseradish-spiked Crème Fraîche (page 144) or natural ketchup for the kids and serve with sliced tomatoes and freshly baked bread for a simple wholesome green-food meal fresh from the garden, farmers market, or your weekly CSA box.

In a large mixing bowl, mix together the chard and green onions, add the flour and toss to combine.

In a separate bowl, whisk together the eggs or tofu, yeast, shallots, garlic, salt, and pepper. Mix the egg or tofu mixture evenly into the chard, massaging the mass with your hands.

In a well-seasoned 10-inch cast-iron skillet, heat 1 tablespoon olive oil and 1 tablespoon Ghee, making sure to coat the bottom and sides evenly. Place the chard mixture into the greased skillet and gently press to smooth the top. Cover and cook over medium-low heat for 8–10 minutes, or until the bottom browns.

Remove from the heat and run a knife around the outside of the pie to loosen the edges. Lay a flat baking sheet on top of the skillet and with a couple of thick hot-pads, carefully invert the pie onto the tray and remove the skillet. Put the remaining oil and Ghee into the hot skillet and carefully slide the pie back in, with the uncooked side down. Cover and cook an additional 6–8 minutes, or until the pie has set and the veggies are completely cooked. Cut chard pie into wedges and serve hot.

Black Bean Burritos

CHIPOTLE BLACK BEANS

1 cup dried black beans

1 ($1/2$-inch) piece kombu
(see glossary)

1 bay leaf

1 tablespoon coconut
or vegetable oil

1 cup chopped onion

$1/2$ cup chopped celery

$1/2$ cup chopped carrot

$1/2$ cup chopped red bell pepper

2 large poblano chile peppers,
roasted, seeded, and
chopped (about 1 cup)

1 to 2 whole chipotle peppers, dried
or canned in adobe sauce (or
for less spice, just use a small
amount of the canned adobe
sauce instead of the whole chile)

1 tablespoon minced garlic

1 teaspoon cumin seed,
toasted and ground

2 teaspoons finely chopped
fresh oregano

1 teaspoon fresh epazote, optional

1 tablespoon tomato paste

Pinch of nutmeg, preferably
freshly grated

2 teaspoons sea salt

In this recipe, the black beans are infused with the bold flavor of chipotle peppers, a jalapeño that has been smoked and dried, or canned in adobo sauce and epazote, a culinary and medicinal herb widely used in Mexican cuisine for its distinctive flavor. Along with the kombu, epazote is a digestive aid that helps prevent the gastric discomfort that can occur for some after eating beans. This is a meal that can also be made in a solar oven (see glossary). The longer these beans cook, the better they taste—developing a deep, richly flavored pot of savory beans. Whichever way you choose to prepare these meal-sized burritos, they are a delicious and simple meal that can be put together in just a few minutes when the basic ingredients have been prepared in advance.

Sort and rinse the beans thoroughly and place in a large soup pot. Cover with 6 cups of water and soak overnight, or at least several hours, before cooking. Drain the beans in a colander, rinse thoroughly, and return to the soup pot. Cover the soaked beans with at least 2 inches of fresh water and bring to a boil. Turn the heat down and skim any foam off the top with a mesh strainer. Add the kombu and bay leaf and gently simmer for about 1 hour, or until the beans are tender and fully cooked.

While the beans are cooking heat the oil in a large skillet, add the onion, and sauté until translucent. Add the celery, carrot, peppers, and garlic and continue cooking until the veggies are almost tender. Add the cumin, oregano, epazote, tomato paste, nutmeg, salt, and cooked black beans to the sautéed veggies and simmer for at least 30 minutes to marry and deepen the flavors. Adjust the seasoning with more sea salt, chipotle, or adobe sauce to taste. Extra beans can be stored in the refrigerator for up to 1 week, or frozen for another meal.

6 large Whole Grain Tortillas
(page 155) or wraps of choice

$1/2$ pound cotija or Monterey
jack cheese, grated

2 cups cooked brown rice

3 cups South-of-the-Border
Slaw (page 76)

$1^1/2$ cups Salsa Fresca (page 135)

$1/2$ cup Creamy Cilantro
Dressing (page 96)

Roasted Tomatillo Sauce
(page 60), heated

Heat each tortilla briefly on the grill or in a skillet to prevent it from cracking while you roll. Lay the warm tortilla on a flat surface and sprinkle with $1/3$ cup cheese. Spoon $1/3$ cup rice and $1/3$ cup beans on the lower half of the circle, leaving a 1-inch margin around the edge. Top the rice and beans with $1/2$ cup slaw, $1/4$ cup Salsa Fresca, and 1 tablespoon Creamy Cilantro Dressing over all. Lift the bottom edge of the tortilla and roll around the filling, tucking in the sides as you roll. Put each burrito on a warm plate and smother with $1/2$ cup Roasted Tomatillo Sauce. Serve with a basket of corn chips and a bowl of Salsa Fresca on the side.

CHEFS PERSONAL KNIVES

Multigrain Pizza

....

2 cups warm water

5½ teaspoons baker's yeast
   or 2 packages active dry

½ cup corn flour

2 cups unbleached white
   or spelt flour

2 cups whole wheat flour

½ cup semolina

¼ cup extra virgin olive oil

1 teaspoon sea salt

Olive oil, for greasing the bowl

⅓ cup cornmeal, for the
   pizza pan or pizza stone

With a few basic ingredients such as flour, yeast, tomato sauce or pesto, chopped veggies, and a good-quality cheese, fresh pizza is easy to prepare at home. And when made with wholesome organic ingredients and helpful hungry hands, homemade pizza can be put together in short order at a fraction of the cost of take-out. Creativity and personal tastes really come into play when making pizza. I usually like to make pizza in big batches, with different toppings on each one, but sometimes I'll roll out small individual crusts and let everyone assemble their own masterpiece. Either way, everyone loves a pizza night. Serve with a cup of minestrone soup and a big green salad for a wholesome meal that everyone, not just the kids, will enjoy. This simple dough is very user friendly and can also be made into focaccia or calzones and Grill Bread (page 163).

In a large bread bowl, combine the water, yeast, and corn flour. Let the mixture sit for several minutes to activate the yeast. This is a good way to check for freshness of your yeast, if it doesn't bloom and bubble, it won't work and you'll need to replenish your supply. Add the remaining ingredients, mix well and knead for 5–10 minutes, adding only enough flour to keep dough from sticking. Wipe any stuck dough from the sides of the bowl, oil it generously with olive oil and roll the dough around the bowl to evenly coat. Cover with a damp cloth and keep warm while the dough rises and doubles in size, about 1 hour.

Preheat oven to 500 degrees F, or the highest temperature it will reach.

Punch down the dough, divide into several balls depending on the size pizzas you are making, and let it rest for 5 minutes before rolling. Press each piece into a flat disk, place on a cornmeal-dusted pizza pan, let rest for a couple of minutes; then roll and carefully stretch the dough into a free-form circle between ⅛–¼ inch thick. Spread the top of the dough with your favorite sauce or pesto, leaving a ¼-inch border around the edge. Cover with cheese and arrange the toppings of choice evenly over the top. Bake for 10–15 minutes, or until the crust is golden and the cheese bubbly. Remove hot pizza from oven and let it sit for a minute before cutting to keep the cheese and toppings from oozing off the pieces.

Big Batch Pizza

....

6 cups warm water

$5^1/_2$ tablespoons baker's yeast
or 6 packages active dry

$4^1/_2$ cups corn flour or masa harina

$4^1/_2$ cups whole wheat flour

$4^1/_2$ cups unbleached
while or spelt flour

$1^1/_2$ cups semolina

$3/_4$ cup extra virgin olive oil

1 tablespoon sea salt

$1/_2$ cup cornmeal, for the
pizza pan or pizza stone

Follow recipe for Multigrain Pizza on facing page, use immediately or roll, double-wrap, and freeze the dough for a quick pizza anytime.

TOPPING SUGGESTIONS
- Sun-Dried Tomato Sauce (page 58), white onion, asparagus, and fresh goat cheese
- Cilantro Pine Nut Pesto (see Garden Pesto, page 136), artichoke hearts, fresh tomato, and Manchego cheese
- Sun-Dried Tomato Sauce, portobello mushrooms, red bell pepper, roasted garlic, fresh ricotta, and Asiago cheese
- Basil Pistachio Pesto (see Garden Pesto, page 136), Italian sausage, fresh tomato, mozzarella, and Pecorino Romano cheese

CALZONE VARIATION:
Calzones are simply a folded over pizza, stuffed instead of topped. Dough is wrapped around fillings in almost every culture and there are many recipes for Indian samosas, Latin empanadas, Russian pirozhki, Chinese dim sum, English pasties, and American turnovers that have been handed down from generation to generation. These tasty little bundles can be made with many different styles of dough, and both yeasted and savory piecrust recipes can be used, depending on what you're making and what's on hand. Italian inspired turnovers are traditionally filled with cheese, meat, and a variety of vegetables—simple meals that are easy to make and perfect to pack and go. Stuff calzones with your favorite pizza toppings or wrap around any sweet and savory fillings you like. Below are a just few different ethnic ideas to help get your creative juices flowing.

- Italian: broccoli, ricotta, and smoked mozzarella
- Mediterranean: roasted seasonal veggies with fresh herbs and feta
- Indian: curried veggies, red beans or lentils, and brown basmati rice
- Mexican: black beans, corn, and pepper jack
- English: turkey, beef or pork, onions, cabbage, and sharp cheddar
- Oriental: stir-fry veggies with meat, poultry, or tofu
- American: add a little sucanat or other sweetener to the dough and substitute the olive oil with Ghee, or coconut oil. Stuff the sweetened dough with thinly sliced apples, or your favorite fresh fruit pie filling.

See following page for Focaccia Variation.

FOCACCIA VARIATION:

Focaccia is like a pizza, but with less stuff on top so the dough can easily rise while baking. It is rolled thicker than a pizza and dimpled with the tips of your fingers, giving this bread a traditional look by making little pockets for the oil and toppings to nest into. The pizza dough recipe makes wonderful focaccia, and substituting milk for the water makes for a slightly chewier texture, as well as added nutrients. My favorite focaccia topping is a combination of fresh seasonal herbs, sun-dried olives, thinly sliced sweet onions, and a sprinkling of Pecorino Romano cheese.

How to Prepare Artichokes

Trim off the end of the stem and any withered or old looking leaves. Cut approximately 1 inch off the top and snip the points off of the remaining leaves with a pair of scissors. Rinse artichokes under cold running water, the commercial chemicals used to grow artichokes can be toxic, so wash them well if they aren't organically grown. In a small bowl, mix together 1 tablespoon lemon juice and water and dip each artichoke into the mixture to keep them from discoloring. Place prepared artichokes and the lemon water in a large steamer with a tight-fitting lid, adding enough water to last throughout the cooking time, if necessary. Artichokes can vary considerably in texture from crop to crop and cooking times will change accordingly. Steam large artichokes for approximately 40 minutes, or until tender. Check for doneness by piercing the bottom with a fork or knife. They are done when the thickest part is tender.

Granny's Stuffed Artichokes

4 large artichokes,
  prepared for cooking

STUFFING

1/4 cup minced shallots

1 tablespoon minced garlic

1 tablespoon extra virgin olive oil

1 tablespoon melted Ghee (page
  150) or unsalted butter

2 cups whole grain bread crumbs
  (sourdough is especially
  good in this recipe)

1/2 cup grated Asiago, Pecorino
  Romano, or Parmesan cheese

1/2 cup pine nuts

1/4 cup chopped Italian parsley

2 tablespoons chopped
  fresh oregano

2 tablespoons chopped
  fresh basil, optional

1/4 teaspoon lemon zest

1/4 teaspoon sea salt

Freshly ground pepper, to taste

2 cups hot water

The weather on the central California coast creates the perfect conditions for growing globe artichokes. From the petite babies, so tender they can be eaten whole, to the extra-large ones that when stuffed can become a full meal. Regardless of size, the freshest and most flavorful artichokes will be dark green, heavy, and firm, and when squeezed, give a little squeak. Artichokes are a great source of good-for-you green food and organically grown ones are always your best choice for flavor and nutrition. The easiest way to prepare artichokes is to simply steam them until tender. To eat, dip the leaves in aioli, Mayonnaise (page 139), or melted butter and scrape the yummy flesh off the end with your teeth. In this recipe, big artichokes are stuffed with bread crumbs, pine nuts, garlic, and cheese, in a traditional Italian dish that was served by my grandmother for special occasions. These showy globes make for a beautiful presentation and are a perfect entrée for the vegetarians in your life when meat is on the menu for others.

Preheat oven to 350 degrees F.

Steam the artichokes until tender, approximately 40 minutes, and set aside to cool. While the artichokes are steaming, prepare the stuffing.

In a small skillet over medium heat, sauté the shallots and garlic in the olive oil for 2 minutes. Add the Ghee and cook for 1–2 minutes, or until the shallots are translucent. Remove from the heat and toss in a large mixing bowl with the remaining stuffing ingredients until combined.

Place the steamed artichokes into a baking dish and gently spread the leaves, carefully pulling out the small center cone, and with a spoon, scrape out the fuzz underneath. You will have a nice pocket to pile in the stuffing, using the tender heart of the artichoke as a bed. Carefully spoon the mixture into the center cavity and between the leaves of the artichoke. Pour the hot water into the bottom of the baking dish and bake for 20 minutes, or until the top is golden brown and the stuffing is nice and hot. This dish is wonderful with just the stuffing to flavor the leaves, but can also be served with lemon butter, aioli, or your favorite dipping sauce on the side for those who also love to dip.

Lima Bean, Shiitake, and Winter Vegetable Stew

1 cup dried baby lima beans

4 cups water

1 (3-inch piece) kombu

1 cup chopped onion

1 tablespoon extra virgin olive oil

2/3 cup sliced carrot

2/3 cup sliced celery

2/3 cup (1/2-inch pieces) yam

1/2 cup sliced fresh shiitake
   mushrooms or rehydrated dried

1 tablespoon mushroom powder

1 tablespoon minced garlic

1/4 cup diced sun-dried tomatoes

2 fresh bay leaves or 1 dried

1 tablespoon chopped fresh thyme

1/2 teaspoon finely chopped sage

1 tablespoon chopped fresh oregano

1 to 2 teaspoons sea salt

Pinch of cayenne

1/4 cup chopped fresh Italian parsley

Baby lima beans, often called butter beans because of their rich flavor and creamy texture, are one of my favorite legumes. In this recipe, hearty winter root vegetables, earthy mushrooms, and garden fresh herbs infuse a rich flavor into this satisfying dish that warms body and soul. Thyme, oregano, sage, and parsley are hearty plants that thrive on regular harvesting and are some of the best herbs for beginning gardeners to cultivate at home. Excellent quality fresh herbs can also be found at farmers markets or in specialty produce sections of most grocery stores. This recipe is perfect for making in a clay cooker (see glossary). The flavors develop into an especially rich dish when prepared using this ancient cooking technique that is still used throughout much of the world today.

Using a large tray, slowly slide the beans from side to side and sort through them, removing any rocks, dirt clods, and broken or misshapen beans. Rinse beans well, place in a bowl, cover with several inches of water, and soak them overnight, or at least several hours for proper digestion. Rinse the beans again, put in a large saucepan, add the water and kombu. Bring to a boil, lower the heat to a simmer, and cook until the beans are tender, about 45 minutes to 1 hour.

In a heavy-bottom soup pot, sauté the onion in the oil until translucent, about 5–6 minutes, add the carrot, celery, and yam and continue cooking for another 5 minutes, stirring frequently. Add the mushrooms, mushroom powder, and garlic and cook a few minutes more, or until the mushrooms are wilted. Add the sun-dried tomatoes, bay leaves, thyme, sage, oregano, salt, cayenne, and cooked limas, along with the remaining water, to the vegetable mixture. Gently simmer for 20–30 minutes to develop the flavor, stirring frequently and adding a little more water, as needed, to prevent scorching. Serve with Kale and Sea Vegetable Salad (page 87) and freshly baked bread.

Broccolini, Mushroom, and Provolone Strata

2 tablespoons extra virgin olive oil

$1/2$ cup finely chopped shallots

1 tablespoon minced garlic

2 cups sliced crimini or
   button mushrooms

4 cups (1-inch cubes) dry crusty
   whole grain or sourdough bread

2 cups (1-inch pieces)
   broccolini florets

$1/4$ cup chopped fresh Italian parsley

1 tablespoon chopped fresh oregano

1 tablespoon chopped fresh basil

1 teaspoon chopped fresh thyme

$1^1/2$ cups coarsely grated provolone

$1/2$ cup grated Parmesan

4 eggs

4 cups whole milk

1 tablespoon Dijon mustard

1 teaspoon sea salt

$1/8$ teaspoon freshly ground
   white pepper

As a young girl, I made a more traditional version of this dish with my Italian-born grandmother with white bread, spicy sausage, seasonal vegetables, and grated Parmesan cheese. On Saturday night we would put the strata together in her special baking dish with the colorful design on the sides and put it in the refrigerator until after church on Sunday, when she would pop it in the oven, creating a wonderful aroma throughout the house. This recipe is one of my own versions of this comforting dish made with whole grain bread and fresh broccolini, a thin long-stemmed, mild-flavored, and tender broccoli, fresh herbs, and a smoky provolone cheese—a reflection of my grandma's love and teachings.

In a large skillet, heat the oil and sauté the shallots and garlic for 2 minutes, stirring constantly. Add the mushrooms and continue cooking until they begin to brown. Remove the mushrooms from the heat and set aside. Place the bread cubes in a large mixing bowl. Add the mushrooms, broccolini, herbs, and cheeses and toss to combine.

In a medium-size mixing bowl, briskly whisk the eggs until light. Add the milk, mustard, salt, and pepper and blend well. Evenly distribute the bread, vegetable, and cheese mixture in a well-greased 9 x 13-inch baking dish. Slowly pour the egg mixture over top and wiggle the custard into the rest of the ingredients until evenly saturated. Cover and let sit for 30 minutes–1 hour, or refrigerate overnight. This allows the bread to fully absorb the custard before being baked.

Preheat the oven to 350 degrees F.

Bake the strata, uncovered, for 40–50 minutes or until the top is golden brown and the center is set. Test for doneness by inserting a sharp knife in the center; if it comes out clean, it is done. If the knife still has egg clinging to the blade, return to the oven and continue baking until it comes out clean and the center is fully set. When done, remove the Strata from the oven and let sit for several minutes before cutting and serving.

Veggie Loaf

1$^{1}/_{2}$ cups finely chopped onion

2 tablespoons extra virgin olive oil

1 cup finely chopped celery

1$^{1}/_{2}$ cups grated carrot

$^{3}/_{4}$ cup chopped fresh mushrooms

1 tablespoon minced garlic

2 cups cooked lentils, cooled

1$^{1}/_{2}$ cups rolled oats

$^{1}/_{2}$ cup chopped pecans or almonds

$^{1}/_{2}$ cup sunflower seeds

$^{1}/_{2}$ cup pumpkin seeds

1 teaspoon finely chopped
fresh sage

2 teaspoons finely chopped
fresh thyme

$^{1}/_{2}$ cup chopped Italian parsley

3 eggs or substitute $^{1}/_{2}$ cup
blended tofu for vegan version

3 tablespoons rehydrated
and puréed sun-dried
tomatoes or tomato paste

3 tablespoons nutritional yeast

1 tablespoon Bragg's liquid
aminos or tamari

1 tablespoon natural
Worcestershire sauce

1 teaspoon sea salt

$^{1}/_{4}$ teaspoon pepper

1$^{1}/_{2}$ cups grated sharp cheddar
cheese, or omit for vegan version

At Esalen, when we make meatloaf with ground beef or turkey, we also make a veggie version, with each chef creating their own signature combination of ingredients. This is one dish that begs for creativity from the cook, and, over the years, I have made these loafs in many different ways. Veggie loaves can be made from a variety of legumes, grains, nuts, and seeds and embellished with herbs, cheeses, and leftovers for added flavor and good texture. Experiment with different ingredients and flavor accents to suit your tastes, the season, and the occasion, creating your own signature veggie loaf. Serve with Chanterelle Gravy (page 63) or Tahini-Miso Gravy (page 64), steamed potatoes or brown rice, and a fresh green salad for a comforting, wholesome, and delicious meal.

Preheat oven to 350 degrees F.

In a large skillet, sauté the onion in the oil until translucent, add the celery, and cook for 2 minutes.

In a large mixing bowl, combine the onion mixture with the carrot, mushrooms, garlic, and lentils. Add the rolled oats, nuts, seeds, and herbs and toss again.

In a small bowl, whisk together the eggs, tomato paste, nutritional yeast, aminos, Worcestershire sauce, salt, and pepper. Add the egg mixture to the other ingredients and mix well. Place 1 cup of the mixture in a food processor and process into a sticky glue-like substance. Combine the veggie glue and cheese with the other ingredients and mix thoroughly. Generously grease 2 loaf pans, or ovenproof dish of choice, and press or shape the mixture into loaves, smoothing the tops as you go. Bake for 50 minutes, or until set and golden brown. Remove from oven and cool for at least 10 minutes before turning out onto a platter. Let the loaf sit for several minutes before cutting for nice even slices. Store in the refrigerator for up to 1 week. This loaf also freezes well and can be defrosted, sliced, and grilled for a great sandwich or vegetarian entrée.

VEGGIE BURGER VARIATION:

Shape the mixture into patties; press both sides with dry bread crumbs, cornmeal, or ground flax seeds, and sauté in a hot skillet with a little oil or Ghee until golden brown on both sides.

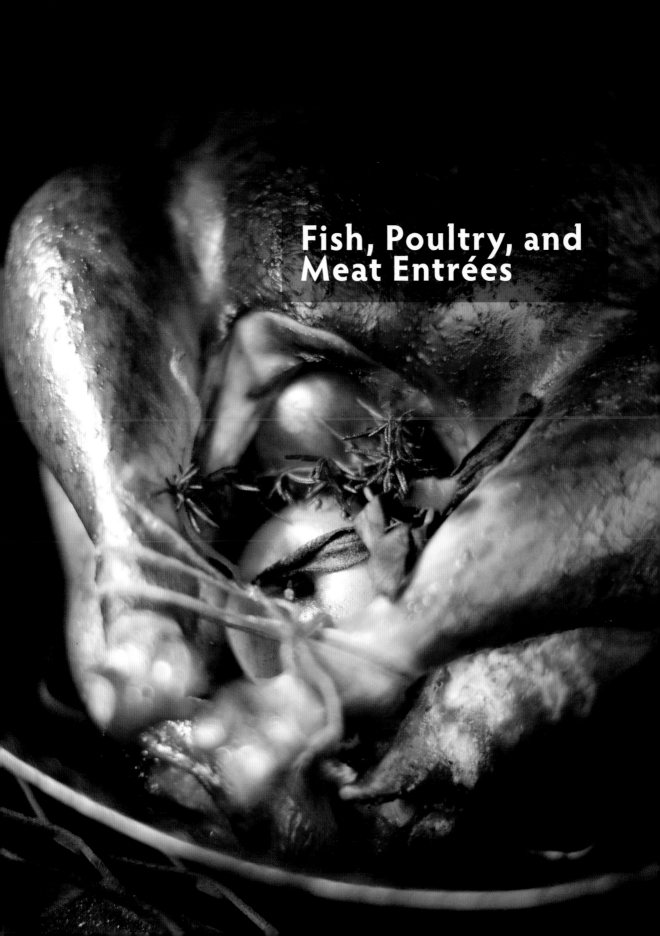

Fish, Poultry, and Meat Entrées

Grilled Whole Fish

FRESH CHILE RUB

1 tablespoon melted coconut oil

2 fresh jalapeños, minced

1 serrano or habañero,
    minced, optional

1 tablespoon minced garlic

$1/4$ cup fresh lime juice

1 teaspoon chili powder

1 teaspoon cumin, toasted
    and ground

1 teaspoon coriander

1 teaspoon sea salt

$1/2$ cup roughly chopped cilantro

FRESH HERBAL RUB

1 tablespoon extra virgin olive oil

1 tablespoon minced garlic

$1/4$ cup chopped dill, basil,
    chervil, or thyme

$1/4$ cup chopped parsley or cilantro

2 tablespoons chopped
    rosemary or sage, optional

$1/4$ cup fresh lemon juice

1 teaspoon lemon zest

1 teaspoon sea salt

1 fresh whole fish, cleaned, scaled,
    and gutted (about 5 to 6 pounds)

1 banana leaf or large Swiss
    chard, kale, or collard leaves

1 lemon, cut into wedges

When cooking for a crowd, grilling a whole fish over hot coals is a simple and festive way to honor the catch of the day. Here are two very different ways to season whole fish. The first one is rubbed inside and out with a fresh chile sauce that nicely spices the smoky flesh. The other preparation is with a savory blend of fresh herbs, lemon, and garlic—my favorite garden seasonings.

I like to calculate $1/2$ pound of fish fillet per person, and I double the weight when serving a whole fish, to account for the skin and bones. Plan on 1 pound of whole fish per person, more or less depending on the variety and size of the fish.

To make the rubs, combine all of the ingredients from your rub of choice in a bowl, blend well, and set aside while you prepare the fish.

Wash and dry the fish inside and out, and with a sharp knife, make several diagonal slits along each side. Place the fish in the center of a large banana leaf, or several big Swiss chard, kale, or collard leaves, and rub the seasoning on both sides, into the slits, and inside the cavity of the fish. Wrap the banana leaf, or several layers of greens, around the fish until it is completely enclosed. Place the wrapped fish on a large sheet of heavyweight aluminum foil, wrap it around the fish a couple of times, folding in the ends, and secure to hold the leaves in place. Alternately, you can wrap and secure the leaves with a lightweight wire and omit the aluminum foil.

Carefully lay the bundle over medium-hot coals and cook for 8–30 minutes on each side, depending on the size of the fish. Remove from the grill and unwrap the foil. Place the leaf-wrapped fish on a big platter, make a shallow slit along the top of the leaves and carefully unveil the fish. Check for doneness by piercing the thickest part of the meat; if your timing was good, the flesh should separate from the bone easily and be flaky. If not, rewrap the fish in leaves and foil, return it to the grill, and continue cooking for several minutes longer, or until done. Serve with lemon wedges on the side.

Grilled Wild Salmon Fillet
with Thai Cilantro Pesto

MAKES 4–6 SERVINGS

GLAZE

1 tablespoon honey

1 tablespoon tamari

1 wild salmon fillet, with the skin
  left on (about 2 to 3 pounds)

1 cup Thai Cilantro Pesto (page 137)

Lemon wedges

This is a simple recipe for cooking a whole fish fillet on the grill, seasoned with a fresh pesto and perfect for both beginners and seasoned chefs looking for an elegant, interesting, and nutritious meal. I like to calculate $1/2$ pound of fillet per person.

Cooking salmon over an open fire is a wonderful technique for this succulent pink-fleshed fish. High in quality protein, omega-3 fatty acids, and other essential nutrients, wild salmon is gaining in popularity, and today these magnificent creatures are being threatened by pollution and over fishing. Please purchase only sustainably caught wild salmon to help preserve this wholesome native food for generations to come.

In a small bowl, combine the honey and tamari and blend well. Brush the flesh side of the salmon fillet with the glaze.

On a well seasoned and oiled grill, place fillet, skin side down, above medium coals and cook until the thickest part is still slightly pink in the center, about 10–20 minutes, depending on the thickness of the fillet. The residual heat will finish off the cooking and the fish will be moist and perfectly done.

Leaving the skin on the grill, use a couple of large spatulas to carefully lift the fillet on to a warm serving platter. Spread Thai Cilantro Pesto evenly over the top of the grilled fillet and serve with lemon wedges on the side.

Back before big fishing boats diminished the coastal rockfish population, local commercial fishermen were able to catch fish in a sustainable and honorable way—with hook, line, and sinker—from small boats launched through the surf early each morning. They took pride in their work and honored the day's catch with special attention to detail as each fillet was carefully removed from the skin and bones, or pinned, a technique for ensuring a boneless serving from each piece. For ease, and especially when serving young children, ask your friendly fishmonger to please pin the fillets, and if in doubt, ask to smell the pieces before purchasing—how else will you know if it is fresh?

Baked Fish Fillet with Fresh Herb Crust

MAKES 6 SERVINGS

6 (about 6 to 8 ounces each) fresh snapper fillets

3 tablespoons unsalted butter, melted, divided

1 tablespoon minced shallots

2 teaspoons minced garlic

$1/4$ teaspoon sea salt

Freshly ground pepper, to taste

$1^1/2$ cups dry whole grain and/or sourdough bread crumbs

1 teaspoon lemon zest

$1/2$ cup finely minced fresh garden herbs*

Lemon wedges

Red snapper, lingcod, or any other light and tender fish fillet will work fine for this recipe. The whole grain savory topping is a low-fat alternative to frying and creates a moist and flavorful fillet. This recipe is very easy to prepare and serve, making it a perfect choice for feeding a crowd, leaving you time to enjoy your family or guests. Be creative, use whatever herbs are in season and calling to be picked from your garden, or look for fresh bundles at the farmers market or grocery store produce section.

Preheat the oven to 450 degrees F.

Wash and dry the fish fillets and place them in a large ovenproof baking dish that has been greased with 1 teaspoon of the butter. Combine remaining butter, shallots, garlic, salt, and pepper in a small saucepan and sauté for 1 minute, stirring constantly. Remove from heat and mix with the bread crumbs, lemon zest, and fresh herbs.

Spoon bread crumbs carefully over each fish fillet and bake for 10–15 minutes, or just until the thickest part of the fillet begins to turn opaque in the center. The fish will continue cooking after it comes out of the oven, from the residual heat, and will be perfectly done when you actually sit down at the table and eat. Serve with lemon wedges on the side.

*Try using mild-flavored herbs like Italian parsley, cilantro, basil, chives, dill, oregano, thyme, marjoram, and chervil. If using stronger flavored herbs like rosemary, sage, tarragon, and sorrel, use less.

A SAMPLE COMBINATION OF FRESH HERBS:

- $1/4$ cup chopped Italian parsley
- 2 tablespoons finely chopped fresh basil
- 1 tablespoon finely chopped fresh thyme
- 1 tablespoon finely chopped fresh dill
- 1 tablespoon finely chopped fresh oregano
- 1 teaspoon finely chopped fresh rosemary

Garden Herb and Lemon Chicken

MAKES 4–6 SERVINGS

1 (4 to 5-pound) whole organic free-range chicken

2 tablespoons extra virgin olive oil

1 teaspoon sea salt

1 tablespoon nutritional yeast

$1/2$ teaspoon lemon zest

Freshly ground pepper, to taste

3 (4-inch) sprigs each rosemary, sage, and thyme

$1/2$ bulb garlic, separated, smashed, and peeled

1 to 3 organic thin-skinned whole lemons, depending on size

A cook at Esalen first introduced me to this technique and it reminded me of the chicken my grandmother used to make when I was a child. Whole lemons and fresh herbs are stuffed into the chicken, and then it is slowly roasted while the flavors permeate the flesh, keeping it moist and delicious. I like to make this dish in a covered ceramic roaster with big chunks of potatoes, carrots, onions, mushrooms, and winter squash baked along with the chicken—so simple and so yummy! Roasted or cooked in a ceramic clay cooker (see glossary), the fresh herbs and tart lemon flavors are what sets this recipe apart from the rest with the promise of a moist and flavorful bird every time.

Preheat oven to 450 degrees F.

Wash chicken, inside and out, dry with paper towels, and place on a rack in an ovenproof baking dish.

In a small mixing bowl, combine the olive oil, salt, yeast, zest, and pepper. Rub the mixture on the inside and outside of the bird and stuff half of the herbs and half of the garlic in the cavity of the chicken. Add the whole lemon, or lemons, and surround with the remaining herbs and garlic, squeezing the sprigs between lemon and flesh.

Place the stuffed chicken in the oven for 10 minutes, then lower the heat to 300 degrees F and roast for 1–1$1/2$ hours, or until done. A free wiggling leg bone and clear running juice is the most accurate test for doneness. Using an instant-read kitchen thermometer that registers 165 degrees F in the thickest part of the thigh meat is another way to be sure it is done. Remove the chicken from the oven and let sit for 10 minutes before cutting to retain moisture in the meat.

Chicken Dijon with Fresh Dill

1/3 cup Dijon mustard

1/4 cup brown or coarse
grain mustard

1/2 cup dry vermouth, or white wine

4 fresh organic free-range chicken
breasts, without skin and bones

2 tablespoons Ghee (page 150)
or olive oil

1/4 cup minced shallots

1/2 cup heavy cream

1/4 cup chopped fresh dill or
2 tablespoons dried

Sea salt and freshly ground pepper,
to taste

4 sprigs fresh dill, optional

This delicious chicken dish had its humble beginnings as a weekend special at our family's first restaurant, the Carmel Café. Over the years the recipe has evolved, and these days I'm inspired to make chicken, turkey, tempeh, or whatever Dijon when the big bouquets of fresh dill arrive at the farmers market each spring. This simple preparation honors this delicate and flavorful herb by bathing it in a tangy mustard-infused white wine sauce. The preparation is easy, even for a novice cook, and can be made from start to finish in just a few minutes for a quick and delicious entrée. Dried dill weed is a good second choice in this recipe, but fresh dill is by far the best choice for great flavor, and can be found in most grocery store produce sections.

In a small mixing bowl, blend the Dijon and brown mustards with the vermouth and set aside. Wash and dry the chicken thoroughly.

In a large skillet, sauté the chicken breasts in the Ghee for 2–3 minutes on each side until lightly browned. Add the shallots and shake the skillet to sauté, along with the chicken, being careful not to burn the pieces, about 1–2 minutes. Deglaze the bottom of the pan with the mustard and wine mixture and stir to blend. Lower the heat, cover, and simmer for 5–8 minutes, or until the chicken is fully cooked in the thickest part. Remove the pieces from the skillet, place on a warm plate and cover to keep hot.

In a small bowl, combine 1/2 cup of the hot mustard sauce with the cream to temper. Stir the dill into the mixture. Blend the creamy dill mixture into the skillet and add the chicken, coating the pieces completely with the sauce. Gently heat over low, being careful not to let the sauce boil. Taste and adjust the seasoning with sea salt and freshly ground pepper. Spoon sauce over each breast as you serve and garnish with a sprig of fresh dill.

Turkey Loaf

MAKES 4–6 SERVINGS

....

1$\frac{1}{4}$-pound free-range organic
    ground turkey (a mixture of
    light and dark meat is best)

1 cup finely chopped onion

$\frac{1}{2}$ cup finely chopped celery

$\frac{1}{2}$ cup diced carrot

$\frac{1}{4}$ cup diced red bell pepper

$\frac{1}{3}$ cup finely chopped
    fresh mushrooms

1 tablespoon minced garlic

1 teaspoon sea salt

$\frac{1}{4}$ teaspoon freshly ground pepper

2 teaspoons natural Worcestershire
    sauce or tamari

$\frac{1}{3}$ cup finely chopped fresh parsley

1 teaspoon finely chopped fresh
    sage or $\frac{1}{2}$ teaspoon dried

2 teaspoons finely chopped fresh
    marjoram or 1 teaspoon dried

$\frac{1}{4}$ cup rehydrated and minced sun-
    dried tomatoes or natural ketchup

1 cup whole grain bread crumbs

2 eggs, lightly beaten

GLAZE

$\frac{1}{3}$ cup natural ketchup

1 tablespoon honey

The preparation for this recipe is easy, and even a novice cook can create a wonderful meal with this tasty loaf as the center attraction. Serve with steamed or mashed potatoes and a green salad for a satisfying and comforting home-cooked meal that is sure to please and nourish.

Preheat oven to 400 degrees F.

In a large bowl, combine all of the ingredients except the glaze until well mixed. Form into a 9 x 5-inch oval loaf in a lightly oiled 13 x 9-inch ovenproof baking dish.

In a small bowl, combine the ketchup and honey and blend well. Brush the top of the loaf with the glaze and bake for 50–60 minutes, or until a thermometer inserted in the center registers 170 degrees F. To retain moisture, let the meatloaf rest for 5 minutes before cutting and serving.

Smoked Turkey with Maple-Herb Brine

MAKES 8–10 SERVINGS

1 (12 to 15-pound) organic turkey

BRINE

2½ gallons hot water

1½ cups maple syrup

1 cup sea salt

2 whole bay leaves

10 cloves garlic, peeled and mashed

1 cup roughly chopped fresh sage

1 cup roughly chopped fresh thyme

1 cup roughly chopped
    fresh Italian parsley

½ cup fresh oregano or marjoram

½ cup fresh rosemary

1 teaspoon freshly ground
    white pepper

RUB

4 tablespoons Ghee (page 150)
    or olive oil

2 teaspoons sea salt

2 teaspoons paprika

2 tablespoon nutritional yeast

SEASONING MIXTURE

1 cup chopped apple

1 cup chopped onion

1 to 2 whole lemons

Several large sprigs of sage, thyme,
    rosemary, oregano, and parsley

Smoking a turkey is an act of love and best reserved for special occasions. When you want an entrée that is easy to serve and will leave you with more time to visit with friends and family, or tend to last minute side dishes, this is the one. Soaking a whole turkey in brine and slowly smoking it over hot coals is an excellent way to ensure a moist and tender outcome.

Our family uses a big Japanese ceramic smoker, but with care, any kind of barbecue with a lid can produce good results. The key is in maintaining a low fire, which takes a bit of practice. If you're not using a gas grill, a charcoal starter is a helpful tool to start the extra coals or wood chips (we like to use fruit wood cuttings and oak bark for extra flavor) that will be needed to keep the fire fed throughout the many hours it takes to finish the smoking process. Don't worry, if your fire doesn't last for the full time needed to finish cooking the meat, or you're just tired of tending the fire for hours—just pop the partially smoked turkey in a 250–300-degree F oven until it is done. You'll still enjoy a tender juicy bird, fragrant with herbs and a rich smoky flavor, but with less fuss. Serve with Chanterelle Gravy (page 63) and traditional Thanksgiving side dishes for a meal to remember.

Wash the turkey inside and out and dry well with a paper towel.

Combine all the brine ingredients in a large pot and stir until the salt is dissolved. Place turkey in a container that will allow it to stay submerged in the brine, a deep soup pot or food-grade bucket works well for this, and pour in the brine. Cover turkey and refrigerate 24–36 hours. (Tip: place the turkey in a big insulated cooler with ice and save the refrigerator space.) When you are ready to begin smoking the turkey, remove it from the brine, rinse inside and out with fresh water and dry well.

Place the turkey breast side up on a wire rack in a roasting pan that will fit into your smoker or barbecue. In a small bowl, combine the rub ingredients and rub the inside and outside of the turkey with the seasoned paste. Toss the Seasoning Mixture in a bowl and fill both cavities loosely. Truss, securing the openings with skewers or a needle and thread, and place a meat thermometer in the thickest part of the thigh flesh. Put the turkey into a 400-degree F smoker or barbecue for about 30 minutes, bring the temperature down to 240–260 degrees F

and maintain that temperature throughout the smoking time. Cook for about 30 minutes per pound, or until the meat thermometer reads 165 degrees F, approximately 6–7 hours for a 12–15 pound turkey. Remove the turkey from the smoker when it is done and let sit for 20 minutes before carving to ensure a moist and flavorful bird.

ROASTING VARIATION:
Preheat oven to 325 degrees F and roast turkey for about 20 minutes per pound for all, or part of the cooking time.

Grass-Fed Beef and Mushroom Stroganoff

MAKES 4 SERVINGS

6 tablespoons Ghee
  (page 150), divided

1 pound top sirloin or tenderloin,
  cut into $1/4$ x $2^1/2$-inch strips

$1/4$ teaspoon sea salt

Freshly ground pepper, to taste

$1/3$ cup minced shallots

1 cup sliced crimini or
  button mushrooms

$1/2$ cup sherry, vegetable,
  or beef stock

1 cup Crème Fraîche (page 144)
  or sour cream

$1/8$ teaspoon fresh grated nutmeg

$1/4$ cup chopped Italian parsley

Beef Stroganoff is my father's favorite meal and one of the first things my grandmother taught me to cook when I was a young girl. Numerous cuts of beef can be used for making Stroganoff, but I recommend using top sirloin or tenderloin to ensure a tender outcome. For the best flavor and nutrition, purchase grass-fed beef whenever possible. Studies have shown that cows raised without hormones or antibiotics and allowed to graze on green grass are healthier for our families, as well as the environment. In this recipe, Crème Fraîche is used in place of the traditional sour cream for its rich flavor and ability to withstand breaking at high heats, but either one will do.

In a large skillet over medium-high heat, melt 4 tablespoons Ghee, add the strips of beef in a single layer, and sprinkle with a little of the salt and pepper. Cook for 1–2 minutes, turn the pieces over and cook the other side for another minute or so. The pieces must be cooked quickly, or the meat will toughen. When both sides are brown, remove the beef from the skillet, place on a plate, and set aside. Do this step in two or three batches for the best results.

In the same skillet over medium heat, sauté the shallots in the remaining Ghee for 2 minutes, add the mushrooms, and cook for several minutes, stirring occasionally, until the mushrooms are golden brown. Deglaze the skillet with the sherry or stock. Place $1/2$ cup of the sauce in a bowl and stir in the Crème Fraîche. Add the meat to the mushrooms in the skillet, pour the cream mixture over all, add the nutmeg and stir to combine. Gently heat the Stroganoff until it comes up to temperature, but do not let it boil. Taste the sauce and adjust the seasoning with sea salt and freshly ground pepper to taste, if needed, and stir in the parsley. Serve immediately over egg noodles, brown rice, or mashed potatoes.

Grilled Leg of Lamb with Fresh Mint and Raisin Sauce

1 small boneless leg of lamb (about 3 pounds)

1 cup red wine

$1/3$ cup chopped garlic

$1/2$ cup tamari

$1/4$ cup chopped oregano

$1/2$ cup chopped mint

1 teaspoon freshly ground pepper

1 tablespoon nutritional yeast

$1/4$ cup extra virgin olive oil

$11/2$ cups Fresh Mint and Raisin Sauce (page 162)

Like many of today's families, mine is a diverse bunch. We represent all styles of eating, and out of respect for the vegetarians of the house, as well as the wonderful flavors that only an open fire can do, we cook most of our meats outside on the grill. A favorite spring meal in our home is fresh boneless leg of lamb grilled to perfection, steamed baby asparagus, roasted new potatoes, garden salad, and a fresh mint and raisin sauce served on the side. For the best value, purchase a whole leg of lamb and have the butcher remove the bone and butterfly the meat. Save the bone and add it to the Fresh Vegetable Stock (page 51) for the foundation of a flavorful and nutritious soup the next day.

Trim the lamb of all fat and silver skin and place in a large glass, ceramic, or stainless steel bowl.

In a small mixing bowl, combine the wine, garlic, tamari, herbs, pepper, yeast, and oil. Pour the mixture over the lamb and refrigerate overnight or at least several hours for the flavors to absorb into the meat.

Heat the coals or grill to medium-low. A good way to test the temperature of your fire is to hold your hand about 5 inches above the cooking surface—you should be able to hold it there for 3–4 seconds before it gets too hot. Grill the lamb for approximately 15 minutes per side for medium-rare, turning often and moving around the heat to cook evenly. The center should read 125 degrees F with a meat thermometer when it is ready. Lamb can become dry if it is over cooked, so keep a close eye on it if you like your meat on the rare side. To retain moisture, let the cooked meat rest on a warm platter, loosely covered, for about 10 minutes before cutting. Thinly slice and serve with Fresh Mint and Raisin Sauce on the side.

Embellishments

Fresh Vegetable Platter with Assorted Dips

Seasonal veggie platters are a staple in our home and my children love to dip. To ensure that everyone will happily eat all their veggies, I cut crispy fresh vegetables in easy to eat shapes and serve them with a variety of tasty dips and spreads. It keeps everyone nourished and satisfied while I finish making dinner and our meal begins with a good helping of enzyme-rich raw veggies. I love making big mandala patterns out of the freshest and most exquisite looking and tasting vegetables I can find, especially for special events and caterings. Showcasing the season's bounty with gorgeous colors and interesting shapes makes the table come to life and invites all to enjoy and appreciate fresh veggies, the cornerstone of good health. Serve fresh vegetable platters, with either beautifully cut or whole baby-size veggies along with your choice of the delicious dips, sauces, spreads, and pesto found in this chapter.

Picking and eating fresh vegetables from the garden is heavenly. However, the quality of produce found at farmers markets is excellent and the savings can be considerable compared to the grocery store. Purchasing directly from the farmers who grow our food is at the heart of local farmers markets. With each passing year, I've noticed these weekly gatherings of community become more and more crowded with shoppers building strong, profitable, and sustainable farmers markets across the country. These days, everyone knows that eating fresh raw fruits and vegetables is essential for good health, and we need a good measure of live enzymes every day to properly digest our meals.

MAKING THE PLATTER

Choose an assortment of fresh vegetables and plan on a couple of pieces of each kind of vegetable or about $1/2$ cup assorted veggies, per person. Cut the carrots into sticks, broccoli, and cauliflower in small florets, cucumber and jicama in spears, and red, orange, and yellow peppers into strips. Tender little green beans, snap and snow peas, baby summer squash, green onions, radishes, and cherry tomatoes can be left whole. To make a magnificent mandala, place the dips you want to serve in a pretty bowl in the middle of the platter. Arrange the cut and whole pieces of vegetables, beginning at the outer edge of the platter and working towards the center. Alternate the colors and shapes into an attractive design as you go, nesting the veggies in toward the center bowl in a pretty pattern. Serve with Hummus (page 132), a flavored Mayonnaise made from scratch (page 139), Rockin' Ranch or Green Goddess Dressing (pages 94 or 95), Olive and Sun-Dried Tomato Tapenade (page 134), or your favorite dip or salad dressing.

Hummus

MAKES 2 CUPS

1½ cups cooked garbanzo
    beans, ½ cup cooking liquid
    reserved, or 1 (15-ounce) can,
    drained, reserving the liquid

1 tablespoon minced garlic

½ cup raw tahini, or toasted
    tahini if you prefer a
    stronger sesame flavor

¼ to 1 teaspoon sea salt, use
    less for canned and more
    for fresh-cooked beans

3 tablespoons fresh lemon juice

½ teaspoon lemon zest

⅓ cup chopped Italian
    parsley, optional

Pinch of cayenne

Hummus traditionally comes from the Arab world and has gained popularity with the rise of the natural foods movement in this country. For a party, serve hummus in a pretty bowl with freshly cut or baby vegetables and crackers, bread, or chips in a basket on the side. Hummus can be made with many variations on the original theme. Substitute any white bean for the garbanzos and season your creation with freshly chopped herbs, roasted red bell pepper, sun-dried olives, or whatever flavors strike your fancy.

Put all ingredients, except the parsley, cayenne, and reserved cooking liquid in a food processor with the S-blade attachment and process, adding more cooking liquid in tablespoon increments, if needed, until the texture is smooth and creamy. Stir in the parsley and cayenne and adjust the seasoning, adding a little more lemon, salt, or cayenne to taste. Store in refrigerator for up to 1 week.

How to Cook Dried Beans Sort through 1 to 2 cups of beans (to save fuel, I usually make a big batch and freeze half) and remove any broken, shriveled, or old-looking ones, along with the dirt clods and rocks often found among dried legumes. Place the sorted beans in a big stainless steel soup pot, cover with water and drain to wash off any residual dirt. Put them back into the pot, cover with several inches of fresh water, and let soak overnight, or up to 24 hours, rinsing and replacing the water every 8 hours to prevent souring. The longer you soak dried beans, the shorter the cooking time. When you are ready to begin cooking, drain, rinse, and return the soaked beans to the pot. Cover with several inches of fresh water and bring to a boil. Add a 4–6-inch piece of kombu (see glossary), lower the heat and simmer for 1–3 hours, depending on variety, or until the beans are tender.

Romesco Sauce

¹/₃ cup almonds, raw,
   soaked, or toasted

1 cup chopped roasted red
   or yellow bell pepper

2 tablespoons rehydrated
   sun-dried tomato

1 slice light grain bread,
   hard crusts removed

2 teaspoons minced garlic

2 teaspoons red wine vinegar

¹/₂ teaspoon sea salt

Pinch of cayenne

¹/₄ cup extra virgin olive oil

1 teaspoon fresh rosemary

1 tablespoon fresh oregano

2 tablespoons fresh Italian parsley

This rich and flavorful sauce has its roots in Spanish cuisine and is good with just about everything, especially grilled veggies, fish, poultry, and meat. Simple to make with a food processor and very tasty, Romesco sauce is a perfect dip for raw veggie platters and is also wonderful served as a spread with crackers or freshly baked bread.

Place the almonds in the bowl of a food processor and process until they are ground into a fine meal. Add the remaining ingredients and process until smooth, scraping the sides of the bowl as you go. Store in an airtight container in the refrigerator for up to 1 week.

Olive and Sun-Dried Tomato Tapenade

MAKES 1¹/₂ CUPS

1 cup pitted sun-dried kalamata
  olives, or your favorite variety
  (black olives produce a more
  mild-flavored tapenade)

¹/₂ cup sun-dried tomatoes,
  soaked in hot water until soft

1 tablespoon minced garlic

1 tablespoon lemon juice

¹/₃ cup chopped parsley

¹/₂ teaspoon fresh rosemary
  or 1 teaspoon dried

¹/₂ teaspoon fresh thyme
  or 1 teaspoon dried

1 tablespoon fresh basil
  or 1 teaspoon dried

Sea salt and freshly ground pepper,
  to taste

2 to 3 tablespoons extra
  virgin olive oil

Capers, optional

To pit olives; cover a cutting
board with a clean kitchen towel.
Spread olives in a single layer on
the towel and cover with second
towel. Use a heavy skillet to hit and
smash the olives once or twice,
making sure to hit them all. The
pits and flesh should separate
easily and 2 cups whole olives
should produce about 1 cup pitted.

This spread is a wonderful flavor booster and versatile condiment
that can be used in many ways. Serve tapenade as a garnish for
simple soups or toss with hot pasta, fresh herbs, and a flavorful
cheese for a quick supper. Spread it on grilled vegetables, fish
fillets, chicken breasts, sliced steak, whole grain crackers, or
freshly baked bread and enjoy as a nourishing quick snack or
appetizer.

Place all the ingredients except the olive oil and capers in a food
processor and pulse to form a rough paste, scraping down the sides as
you go. Transfer to a serving bowl and stir in the olive oil and capers, if
using. Taste and adjust the seasoning with a little sea salt and freshly
ground pepper. To store, place in an airtight container, cover with a
little more olive oil, if needed, and keep in the refrigerator for up to
several weeks, depending on the kind of olive used.

Salsa Fresca

MAKES 2 1/2 CUPS

2 cups (1/4 to 1/2-inch pieces)
assorted heirloom, or
other variety, tomatoes

1/2 cup diced red onion

1 fresh jalapeño, minced

1 fresh serrano chile,
minced, optional

1 tablespoon minced fresh garlic

1/2 teaspoon toasted and
ground cumin seed

1/2 teaspoon sea salt

1 tablespoon fresh lime juice

1/3 cup chopped fresh
cilantro, packed

When the tomatoes are heavy on the vine and the farmers markets are overflowing with all the beautiful heirloom varieties, I like to combine a variety of colors, flavors, and textures in a fresh salsa. When purchasing heirloom tomatoes, choose several varieties and sample them throughout the coming week to know what you like and what to buy the next time you shop. Celebrity, Brandywine, Black Krim, Green Zebra, Big Rainbow, Jubilee, and bi-colored Pineapple tomatoes are some of the more common varieties you will find in farmers markets and natural food stores. Using a sharp knife, as well as carefully cutting the tomatoes with the skin side down, will help the delicate vine-ripened tomatoes hold their shape. Serve this enzyme-rich condiment as a dip with corn chips, a garnish for grilled meat, fowl, or fish, or put a scoop in an avocado half and enjoy a fresh and healthy snack.

Combine all of the ingredients in a bowl, gently stir, cover, and let sit at least 10 minutes to marry and deepen the flavors before serving.

Garden Pesto

MAKES 1¹/₂ CUPS

1 to 2 tablespoons chopped
   garlic, to taste

¹/₂ teaspoon sea salt

¹/₂ cup raw cashews, pine nuts,
   almonds, pecans, pistachios,
   macadamia nuts, walnuts,
   pumpkin, or sunflower seeds

4 cups fresh herbs, basil, cilantro,
   arugula, spinach, and/or
   parsley leaves, large stems
   removed and tightly packed

¹/₂ cup extra virgin olive oil

¹/₂ cup finely grated Pecorino
   Romano or Parmesan cheese,
   omit for vegan version

Freshly ground pepper, to taste

Every year when the basil leaves are calling to be harvested, especially before the hot summer days turn them bitter as they try to blossom, we make a lot of pesto. Basil comes in numerous varieties and each one has a slightly different flavor, texture, and color. Genovese, Mammoth, Globe, Cinnamon, Lemon, Purple Thai, and others are easily grown, or can be found in abundance at farmers markets, at least throughout the summer months.

Pesto can also be made from a variety of other fresh greens like cilantro, parsley, spinach, and arugula, blended with a variety of nuts and seeds, depending on what is in season, what is in the larder, and the flavors you want to create. Freshly made pesto is a great way to feed the whole family big bunches of good-for-you green food, especially when tossed with pasta, spread on bread, or as a topping for quinoa or brown rice. For a quick, delicious, and nutritious snack anytime, keep homemade Garden Pesto on hand in the refrigerator and be creative.

In a food processor bowl fitted with an S-blade, combine the garlic, salt, and nuts or seeds of choice and process, scraping the sides of the bowl as you go. Add the herbs or greens of choice in three increments and continue processing while drizzling oil in a stream through the top, scraping the sides as needed. When the pesto is smooth and creamy, add the cheese, if using, and process again. Taste and adjust the seasoning, if needed, with a little more salt and freshly ground pepper to taste.

Thai Cilantro Pesto

$1/2$ cup raw or lightly toasted
cashews, without salt

1 tablespoon minced garlic

2 tablespoons minced lemon grass

2 tablespoons minced gingerroot

1 large kaffir lime leaf, rib removed,
or $1/2$ teaspoon lime zest

$1/2$ teaspoon sea salt

Pinch of cayenne

1 tablespoon freshly
squeezed lime juice

1 teaspoon toasted sesame oil

4 cups chopped fresh cilantro, large
stems removed and packed

$1/2$ cup unrefined sesame
oil, not toasted

The flavors of the orient come alive in this brightly flavored pesto infused with lemon grass, gingerroot, kaffir lime, and creamy cashews. If you can find them, raw macadamia nuts can be substituted for the cashews for a special tropical twist. Cilantro is a powerful green food and a rich source of vitamins, minerals, and antioxidants—vital elements for good health. Current research shows that if eaten in large enough quantities, cilantro helps the body to release toxins, especially heavy metals, and that can affect our well-being. This recipe packs a lot of wonderful green food into each serving and the exotic flavors of this pesto makes it easy to eat a healthy helping. Toss with rice or buckwheat noodles and serve smothered with steamed fresh vegetables, a dollop of pesto, and a sprinkling of Tamari-Toasted sunflower seeds (page 147) for a quick family meal that everyone enjoys.

In a food processor bowl fitted with the S-blade, process the cashews until finely ground. Add the garlic, lemon grass, gingerroot, kaffir lime leaf or lime zest, salt, cayenne, lime juice, and toasted sesame oil and process for 5 seconds. Add the cilantro in batches as you continue processing the mixture into a smooth paste, scraping the side of the bowl as you go. Use immediately or store in the refrigerator for up to one week.

Cranberry-Tangerine Relish

MAKES ABOUT 3 CUPS

1 package organic cranberries, picked through and washed

2 medium-size tangerines, cut into quarters and seeded, or 1 large orange

$1/2$ cup agave nectar or honey

This fresh relish adds a colorful splash, as well as important enzymes for digestion, to our neighborhood Thanksgiving feasts. Cranberries are a seasonal offering we look forward to every fall and use in many ways. A cranberry-pear pie is one of my favorite fall desserts, and for this I'll sometimes use frozen cranberries; however, fresh cranberries are essential for this recipe. At the Café Amphora, we made beautiful fruit tarts with this relish mixture spread over sweetened cream cheese and garnished with red currant jelly–glazed kiwi slices. It was a spectacular presentation that many of our customers who had never tasted fresh cranberries loved and appreciated. At home, I like to layer this refreshing relish with yogurt, sliced bananas, berries, and chopped almonds in a yummy multi-layered parfait. And sometimes, I just eat it with a spoon.

Place the cranberries and tangerines into the food processor with the S-blade attachment and process in pulses, taking care to keep the texture a bit chunky, scraping the sides as you go. Pour the mixture into a stainless steel or glass mixing bowl and stir in the agave nectar until well blended. Taste and add a little more of the sweetener, if needed. Let this relish stand at room temperature for at least 1 hour before serving to develop the flavor. Store any leftovers in a tightly-sealed jar in the refrigerator for 7–10 days.

Mayonnaise from Scratch

MAKES ABOUT 1 2/3 CUPS

2 large egg yolks

1 teaspoon Dijon mustard

2½ tablespoons fresh lemon juice

½ teaspoon sea salt

Pinch of cayenne, optional

1½ cups light oil*, or
  in combination with a
  full flavor oil**

MAYONNAISE VARIATIONS:

• Aioli: fresh minced
  garlic and olive oil

• Remoulade: capers, cornichons,
  Dijon, fresh parsley, chives

• Tartar Sauce: pickles, scallions,
  horseradish, fresh dill, lemon
  juice, and lemon zest

• Thousand Island: chives, green
  and red bell peppers, pickles,
  ketchup, and fresh parsley

• Fresh Herbs, alone or in
  combination: dill, basil,
  tarragon, parsley, cilantro,
  chervil, and chives

• Flavored vinegars (substituted
  for the lemon juice), lemon or
  lime zest, tamari, gingerroot,
  flavored mustards, bottled
  hot sauce, wasabi powder,
  roasted red peppers, anchovies,
  and roasted garlic are other
  flavoring possibilities

Real mayonnaise is made from emulsified egg yolks and oil, flavored with lemon, mustard, salt, and pepper. The commercial versions are full of added ingredients, stabilizers, and preservatives, and can be very expensive. Making mayonnaise is simple and when made from scratch with fresh eggs and quality oil, is a natural low-cost alternative to the choices found on grocery store shelves. This basic recipe can be made very quickly with a food processor and takes only a few minutes longer to do by hand with a whisk and bowl. Either way, this versatile condiment can be enjoyed with a variety of additions, creating custom flavors to complement your favorite foods. Farm-fresh eggs coming from free-range chickens that are fed organically grown food are well worth seeking out from neighbors, or local farmers markets, as they always produce a superior mayonnaise and Hollandaise (page 46). Choose cold-pressed unrefined vegetable oils whenever possible for the best flavor and create your own signature version of this richly flavored, economical, and versatile embellishment.

FOOD PROCESSOR METHOD:

Place all the ingredients, except the oil, into a food processor fitted with the S-blade, or blender on low speed, and process for 30 seconds, scraping the sides as you go. With the machine running, slowly add the oil through the top opening, beginning with one teaspoon at a time. As the mixture thickens, continue adding in small increments until half of the oil is incorporated. Add the remaining oil in a slow steady stream until the mayonnaise is thick and silky. Taste and correct the seasoning with a little more salt or lemon to your liking. Enjoy as is, or experiment with some of the variations listed. Serve immediately, or store in an airtight jar in the refrigerator for 3–4 days.

HAND METHOD:

In a medium-size mixing bowl, whisk the egg yolks until slightly thickened. Stir in the mustard, lemon juice, salt, and cayenne and blend well. Whisk in the oil, 1 teaspoon at a time, until at least half is incorporated into the egg mixture. Continue whisking and add the remaining oil in a thin steady stream until the emulsion is smooth and glossy.

Light oils include rice, canola, rapeseed, almond, safflower, and sunflower.

**Full flavor oils include extra virgin olive, sesame, corn, flax, and walnut.*

Homemade Yogurt

MAKES 3–4 CUPS

1 cup non-instant skim milk powder, optional for a thicker consistency

3 cups whole milk

$^1/_2$ cup yogurt starter (see glossary)

For a special treat, there is nothing quite like yogurt made with warm milk, lovingly stroked from a family cow, complete with all of the healthy enzymes that are destroyed in commercial processing. If you are fortunate enough to have a family cow or a neighbor whose cow gives enough milk to share, by all means use fresh raw milk. There is much misinformation regarding raw, cultured, and other traditional foods. The research shows that we would do well eating more of these foods that nourished our ancestors. The Weston Price Foundation (see glossary) is a good resource for the most current information on these as well as other health related topics.

Live yogurt contains high-quality proteins, minerals, and enzymes that are easily assimilated, often even by those individuals who are sensitive to milk. It introduces beneficial bacteria for digestive health and also contains all of the known vitamins, including D and B-12, important nutrients that are hard to find in most modern diets. I prefer to use organic whole milk when making yogurt for the best flavor and good health. Reduced-fat milk can be substituted with good results, just add the optional powdered milk for the best texture.

If you are using powdered milk, whisk it into the fresh milk until smooth and strain out any lingering lumps before proceeding.

In a large stainless steel pot over medium heat, gently heat the milk, stirring constantly. Check the temperature with an instant read thermometer often and when it reaches 180 degrees F remove the pot from the heat. Cool the milk to 110 degrees F before adding the starter.

In a small bowl, mix together the yogurt starter and 1 cup warm milk to temper. Stir the thinned yogurt into the rest of the milk and mix well. Pour into a sterile wide-mouthed $^1/_2$-gallon jar. Cover, wrap with several layers of thick towel, and nest in a warm place (80–100 degrees F) for 6–8 hours, or overnight to thicken.

Another great way to keep the milk warm enough to culture is to pour it into a wide-mouth 1-quart thermos that is sealed tightly to hold the heat. A good place to culture the yogurt is on a high shelf in a heated room, or in a gas oven with warmth of the pilot. Store freshly made yogurt in the refrigerator for 7–10 days and remember to save a bit for making the next batch.

Yogurt Cheese

MAKES 2 CUPS

....

1 quart plain Yogurt (page 141)

This is a simple, nutritious, and flavorful enzyme-rich cream cheese that can be made overnight and then be ready in the morning for spreading on toast, muffins, or bagels. Because the milk was not heated in the process, yogurt cheese still contains live enzymes and is easier for us to digest than regular cream cheese. Use yogurt cheese as an alternative to sour cream on top of baked potatoes, blended into creamy dips, or for a tangy note in sweet and savory dressings. I like it spread on sandwiches in place of mayonnaise, mixed into salad dressings, or made into a luscious cheesecake and other creamy sweet treats. Making fresh cheese with your own Yogurt is easy, economical, takes only minutes to do.

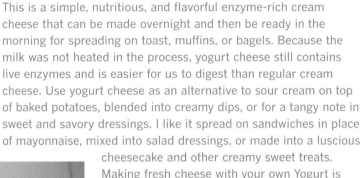

Line a colander with a double layer of cheesecloth, cotton muslin, or a fine-mesh sprouting bag and pour in the yogurt. Let sit about 1 hour to drain off most of the liquid. Tie the corners, or pull the drawstring, and hang the yogurt to drain overnight, with a bowl underneath to catch the drips. In the morning, the cheese will be ready to eat. If you want to flavor your cheese with any additions, place it in a bowl and blend with sea salt, spices, fresh herbs, minced garlic, snipped chives, finely chopped green onion, minced hot or sweet chile peppers, sun-dried tomato or olives pieces, dates, dried fruit, and spices, or your favorite embellishments. Yogurt cheese will keep in the refrigerator for 5–7 days.

Simple Fresh Cheese

1/2 gallon whole cow, goat, or sheep milk, the fresher the better

3 to 5 tablespoons fresh lemon juice, apple cider, or distilled vinegar

From simple fresh cheeses like this one, to pungent inoculated rounds that are aged to perfection, hand-made artisan cheeses come in an amazing array of styles and flavors. This recipe is for a basic farmer's cheese—a versatile soft, fresh-made cheese. If you are fortunate enough to have access to fresh raw milk from well-managed cows or goats, by all means use it. Otherwise, whole organic milk works fine for this recipe.

In a heavy-bottom stainless steel pot, heat the milk to 175 degrees F, stirring constantly to avoid scorching. Remove from the heat and continue to stir the milk while slowly adding the lemon juice or vinegar in 1-tablespoon increments. When you notice the milk begin to curdle, stop stirring, cover, and let sit, allowing the curds and whey to separate. If the curds do not completely set up after 1–2 minutes, add a little more lemon juice until you can see a clear separation of curds and whey. Leaving the whey a little cloudy will produce a softer cheese. For a firmer texture, the whey should be clear.

Pour the curdled milk through a fine-mesh sprouting bag, several layers of cheesecloth, or a piece of cotton muslin that has been placed in a colander with a bowl underneath to catch the whey. Cool for 30 minutes.

Tie the corners of the cheesecloth together and hang the cheese to drain, over a bowl to catch the drips, for 2–3 hours, or until the curds have stopped dripping. Remove the cheese from the cloth and place in a large bowl. This is a mild-flavored fresh cheese, if you want to flavor it with any additions, now is the time. Toss the curds in a bowl with your choice of sea salt, fresh herbs, spices, minced garlic, snipped chives or finely chopped green onion, fresh hot or sweet chile peppers, sun-dried tomato pieces, or chopped olives. For a sweet slant, combine with small pieces of fresh or dried fruit, or your favorite flavor accents. Enjoy fresh cheese when made, or a firmer texture, hang in the cheesecloth for additional 4–6 hours. Store in an airtight container in the refrigerator for 7–10 days, depending on the freshness of your milk.

NOTE: *Whey is full of protein and a health tonic that many enjoy. It can also be incorporated into breads, dressings, and enzyme-rich fermented beverages.*

Crème Fraîche

MAKES 1 CUP

1 cup heavy cream

2 tablespoons buttermilk or freshly cultured crème fraîche

Crème Fraîche is a thick European-style cultured cream with a smooth velvety texture. It is commonly used in soups, sauces, dressings, and dips and has a wonderfully rich and buttery flavor. Unlike sour cream, Crème Fraîche is a live cultured food and will resist breaking when heated. I always begin with the best quality cream I can find. Thankfully I have friends and neighbors who raise livestock and gift me with fresh raw milk when they can. I am always grateful when I can get this local delicacy, but pasteurized organic whole milk cream from the store is what I usually use. Any dairy product labeled whipping cream, cream, or heavy cream will work fine for this recipe. Commercially made Crème Fraîche is quite expensive, so reserve a few tablespoons of each batch you make to use as the starter for the next one.

Combine the cream and buttermilk or Crème Fraîche in a glass jar and cover tightly. Place the jar in a warm spot (about 70 degrees F) for 15–20 hours, or until thick. For the best texture, refrigerate for at least 6 hours before using. Homemade Crème Fraîche will keep refrigerated for up to 2 weeks.

Crispy Tempeh Crumbles

MAKES 1 CUP

....

$1/2$ pound tempeh, cut
　into $1/4$-inch pieces

2 tablespoons coconut, sesame,
　or extra virgin olive oil

$1/2$ teaspoon sea salt

Tempeh (see glossary) is a staple food in my kitchen and this simple recipe embellishes many a meal at our family table. There are numerous varieties and flavors of tempeh on the market and I encourage you to explore them all. The cakes are made from a base of cultured soybeans, and some varieties have added grains, seeds, seaweed, vegetables, and other flavorings. Tempeh has a tendency to absorb a lot of oil when cooked on the stove top and often becomes too greasy for my taste. As an alternative, I've found that baking small pieces with just a little oil in a hot oven produces a nice crunch and perfect texture, without all the grease. This recipe is very easy to prepare and adds a flavorful high protein note to salads, soups, and savory fillings.

When you're feeling creative, or want to slant the flavor of the crumbles in the direction of the other dishes that you are serving, add a touch of chili powder, curry powder, fresh or granulated garlic, exotic spices, or your favorite seasoning to the tempeh bits along with the salt and oil before baking. Fresh herbs should be tossed into the tempeh crumbles when they are removed from the oven in order to preserve their flavor and bright color.

Preheat oven to 350 degrees F.

In a small mixing bowl, toss the tempeh pieces with the oil, salt, and any other seasonings you want to add. Spread evenly in an ovenproof baking dish and bake for 15–20 minutes, stirring occasionally, until they are sizzling and just beginning to brown. Do not over bake the crumbles as the oil will continue to cook the tempeh even after you take it out of the oven—so watch carefully. Crispy Tempeh Crumbles are best served hot or at room temperature. Store in an airtight container in the refrigerator for 5–7 days.

Tamari-Toasted Nuts and Seeds

MAKES 1 CUP

1 cup nuts or seeds (almonds, cashews, pecans, walnuts, pine nuts, hazelnuts, sunflower, or pumpkin seeds)

1 to 2 tablespoons tamari, nama shoyu, or soy sauce

1 teaspoon honey

Lightly toasting nuts and seeds adds another dimension to their natural flavor and also gives them a nice crunch. To retain their freshness, raw nuts and seeds are best stored in the freezer until used. Nuts and seeds can also be soaked overnight to activate the dormant live enzymes then seasoned and dehydrated as a living food alternative to the oven method. Either way you choose, protein-packed nuts and seeds are an important part of a healthy, sustainable diet. Sprinkled on soups, salads, entrées, or just eaten by the handful, tamari-toasted nuts and seeds are delicious, nutritious, and fun whole foods.

Heat oven to 350 degrees F.

Spread the nuts or seeds evenly on a baking sheet and bake until they become fragrant, but before they begin to darken in color, about 8–12 minutes, depending on variety and size of the nuts. Be watchful, roasted nuts will become bitter if over done. Transfer the hot nuts or seeds to a stainless steel or glass mixing bowl, sprinkle with tamari, nama shoyu, or soy sauce, add the honey, and toss with a wooden spoon to coat evenly. Spread seeds out around the bowl and up the sides as thinly as possible and stir frequently until completely cool. Toasted seeds will stay fresh in a tightly sealed jar for about 1 week.

Alternative Live Dehydration Place the nuts or seeds in a bowl, add 1 quart of water, and soak overnight to bring them back to life. In the morning, rinse and drain well before spreading them out on a clean towel to dry. Let air dry for several hours, or hand dry with the towel, and place them in a clean bowl. Sprinkle with tamari, nama shoyu, or soy sauce and honey and toss with a wooden spoon, or hands, to evenly coat before dehydrating.

ELECTRIC DEHYDRATOR METHOD: Spread the mixture evenly over a tray lined with Teflex sheets or parchment paper and dehydrate at 108 degrees F for 10–12 hours or until thoroughly dry and crunchy.

OVEN METHOD: Place the mixture in single layers on baking sheets lined with parchment paper and bake on the lowest temperature setting of your oven, preferably less than 110 degrees F, for 10–12 hours, or until thoroughly dry and crunchy. If your oven has a convection setting—use it—the moving air will speed the drying process, if not, keep the door slightly ajar to encourage air circulation.

Whole Grain Croutons

MAKES 2 CUPS

3 tablespoons olive oil or melted Ghee (page 150)

1 teaspoon minced garlic

$1/4$ teaspoon lemon zest, optional

$1/4$ teaspoon sea salt

$1/8$ teaspoon freshly ground pepper

$1/4$ teaspoon paprika

2 teaspoons nutritional yeast, optional

4 cups (1-inch cubes) whole grain bread, about 4 to 5 thick slices

Every culture has some kind of a recipe for using bread that is past its prime. When the freshness has left the loaf, croutons are simple to make and perfect for a flavorful, crunchy, and an inexpensive garnish. This basic recipe can be embellished with herbs, chili powder, or other seasonings to dress up simple soups and salads, adding a special note that is always appreciated. For seasoned bread crumbs in a flash, just whirl whole-grain croutons in the food processor and store any extra in the freezer for those last minute needs.

Preheat oven to 300 degrees F.

In a medium-size mixing bowl, combine all of the ingredients, except the bread. Add the bread cubes and toss to evenly coat. Put the croutons on a baking sheet in a single layer and bake for 12–20 minutes, depending on the kind of bread you use. Toss several times while baking and remove from the oven when crispy and just beginning to brown. The hot oil will keep cooking the croutons even after they are removed from the oven, so watch carefully. Serve hot as a garnish in soups, or cool completely before adding to salads.

Gomasio

MAKES 1 CUP

1 cup sesame seeds

¼ to ½ teaspoon sea salt

Gomasio, the commonly used table salt in macrobiotic diets, is made from sea salt and ground sesame seeds. This flavorful condiment is an excellent source of calcium and is very easy to make. The ratio of sea salt to sesame seeds is variable; ranging from 1 part salt to 5 parts seeds, or 1 part salt up to 20 parts seeds, depending on personal taste. I love the flavor of toasted sesame seeds and use a high ratio of seeds to salt, sprinkling it generously on eggs, grains, and vegetables for its unique flavor and nutritional benefits.

Traditionally, Gomasio is ground with a wooden pestle in a special bowl called a suribachi, but you can also make it in a hand grinder, food processor, or small electric grinder with good results. This simple and inexpensive condiment gets a nutritional boost with the addition of ground flax seeds, dulse, or cayenne and is a tasty way to garnish cooked grains, soups, and steamed vegetables. Keep a jar on the table and watch it disappear, it is that good!

Place seeds in a dry skillet and toast until they begin to smell fragrant, tossing or stirring constantly for several minutes over medium heat. Do not over toast the seeds. The sesame seeds will continue cooking from the heated oil within, so be sure to remove from the heat before they begin to brown, or pop, or they can become bitter. Pour into a shallow stainless steel bowl, add sea salt, and toss for several minutes. Cool completely. If you don't have a suribachi, pulse the seeds and salt in a food processor or small grinder until about eighty percent of the seeds are ground, stopping before it starts to clump together. Store Gomasio in a wide-mouthed jar with a tight-fitting lid and use within 1 week to ensure freshness.

OPTIONAL ADDITIONS:

- 2 to 4 tablespoons ground flax seeds
- 2 tablespoons ground dulse or other seaweed
- 1 to 2 tablespoons spirulina
- Pinch of cayenne

Ghee

MAKES ABOUT 2 CUPS,
DEPENDING ON THE
BRAND AND QUALITY
OF BUTTER USED

1 pound organic unsalted butter

Cheesecloth or cotton muslin

Heavy-bottom stainless
steel or glass pot

In India, or places where refrigeration is not available, or minimal, Ghee is often used in place of butter. Ghee is made from butter that has had the milk solids removed and can be used in any recipe that calls for clarified butter. It is the milk solids that have a tendency to go rancid, and are also the components of dairy products responsible for most of the digestive problems in those who are sensitive. In my experience, many people with these sensitivities can digest Ghee much easier than butter. Ayruvedic doctors use Ghee as medicine, and in this system of healing, diet is an integral part of their pharmacopoeias. Ghee can help us assimilate the full measure of fat-soluble nutrients from the foods we eat, tastes like essence of butter slightly roasted, and is heavenly on popcorn. Ghee, unlike butter, will not go rancid if handled properly. It does not require refrigeration, and each batch should be eaten within a few weeks, however, I have stored quart jars of organic Ghee in a cooler for several months at a time while on long surfing trips to the tropics and it kept just fine.

In a deep pot, melt the butter over a very low heat, without stirring, and keep simmering until the butter becomes a clear golden liquid, about 15 minutes. Skim the foam off the top and just let the solids settle to the bottom. Remove from the heat while the Ghee is golden in color, before it becomes too dark, and pour carefully through several layers of cheesecloth into a stainless steel bowl to cool. Keep in an airtight wide-mouthed jar or butter crock. Ghee will look cloudy and be semi-solid at room temperature, but does not need to be refrigerated.

Ponzu Sauce

MAKES 1 CUP

½ cup tamari, nama
   shoyu, or soy sauce

⅓ cup freshly squeezed lemon juice

¼ cup mirin

1 tablespoon honey or agave nectar

1 teaspoon lemon zest

Crushed red pepper, optional

Ponzu sauce is a traditional Japanese condiment that is a blend of sweet, sour, and savory flavors. This zesty all-purpose seasoning is good on just about everything. Drizzle it lightly on vegetables, grains, meat, fish, or fowl for a refreshing lift or blend it into dressings or dips as a flavorful accent. For added zing, embellish Ponzu sauce with toasted sesame oil, garlic, gingerroot, or other seasonings of choice.

Place all of the ingredients in a small mixing bowl and whisk until well blended. Pour the sauce into a pretty serving bowl and serve with a small spoon.

Breads

Corn Tortillas

MAKES 12

....

2 cups masa harina or corn flour

¼ teaspoon salt

1 to 1⅓ cups hot water

Tortillas made from scratch are easy with a tortilla press or rolling pin, and with a little practice can be patted flat by hand like the traditional Mexican and Indian cooks do every day. The wonderful flavor and texture of freshly made tortillas is well worth the extra effort, and once you try them, it might be tough going back to eating the commercially made varieties.

In a medium-size mixing bowl, combine the flour and salt and stir in the water until the dough comes together. You might need to adjust the water, depending on the grind of the corn. Make a soft ball of dough by mixing and kneading with your hands for several minutes until it is smooth. Divide the dough into 12 equal parts, rolling each into smooth round balls about the size of a golf ball, and cover with a damp cloth. Lay a piece of waxed paper or plastic on the bottom of a tortilla press and, one at a time, place each ball in the center and press into thin 5–6-inch rounds. An alternative technique is to use a rolling pin. Place each of the balls between two sheets of waxed paper or plastic wrap and evenly roll them into free-formed rounds.

Cook the tortillas over medium-high heat in a well-seasoned or lightly oiled cast-iron skillet, heavy griddle, or Mexican comal for 2–3 minutes on each side, or until they begin to brown. Serve immediately, or wrap warm tortillas in a damp towel and keep in a low oven, or woven tortilla basket with a lid, while you cook the rest. Handmade tortillas are best eaten fresh, but leftovers can be wrapped and refrigerated for several days, or frozen for later use. Heat stored tortillas on a hot griddle to refresh before serving.

Whole Grain Tortillas or Chapatis

MAKES 6–10 DEPENDING ON THE SIZE

2¹/₂ cups whole wheat or spelt pastry flour (unbleached white flour can be substituted for some of the whole grain flour for a lighter variation)

³/₄ teaspoon salt

1 teaspoon aluminum-free baking powder, optional for a lighter texture

3 tablespoons melted coconut oil, Ghee (page 150), or vegetable oil of choice

³/₄ cup water

The popularity of sandwich wraps has raised the tortilla to new heights. Big wraps can be purchased in many styles and flavors from the grocery store, but they can also be made with organic whole grains at home for a fraction of the cost. Called tortillas in Mexico and chapatis in India, these simple unleavened breads are easy to make and a fun food for special family gatherings, especially when you have extra hands to help roll, cook, and stack as you go.

In a mixing bowl, combine the flour, salt, baking powder, if using, and oil or Ghee and rub the mixture together with your fingers to blend. Add water until the dough holds together, you may need to add a little more water depending on the grind and type of flour you are using.

Knead the dough right in the bowl, or on a lightly floured counter top, adding a little dusting of flour as needed, until smooth, about 5 minutes. Cover the bowl and let dough rest for 20 minutes or longer to allow the grains to hydrate and to develop the best texture.

Divide the dough into 10 equal parts, roll each into smooth round balls, and cover with a damp cloth. One at a time, place the balls between two sheets of waxed paper or plastic and with a rolling pin, roll each one evenly into 6–8-inch free-form rounds. If you are making large wraps, divide the dough into 6 parts and roll into 10–12-inch rounds. Cook tortillas over medium heat in a well-seasoned or lightly oiled cast-iron skillet, heavy griddle, or Mexican comal for approximately 2 minutes on each side, or until they begin to brown and puff. Serve immediately, or wrap in a damp towel and keep warm in a tortilla basket or a warm oven while you cook the rest. Wrap and refrigerate any leftovers and use within a few days, or freeze for later use. Heat stored tortillas on a hot griddle to refresh before serving.

Handmade Whole Grain Crackers

MAKES 4 LARGE CRACKERS

2 cups whole wheat pastry flour

1/4 cup rye flour

1/4 cup oat flour

1/4 cup corn flour

1/4 cup garbanzo flour

1 teaspoon sea salt

1/2 cup extra virgin olive or sesame oil, or melted Ghee (page 150)

1 cup water or more, depending on the grains used

1/8 cup natural brown sesame seeds

1/8 cup poppy seeds

1/8 cup caraway seeds

1/8 cup fennel seeds

1/2 cup sunflower seeds, optional

1/2 cup pumpkin seeds, optional

This crunchy whole grain cracker is embellished with an assortment of flavorful seeds and makes a perfect foundation for sliced cheese, meats, or your favorite spreads. Make a weekly batch of these nutritious crackers, at a fraction of the cost of store-bought, and store them in an airtight container for snacking or serving along side soups and salads. This recipe is very forgiving and can be stretched into many variations with the addition of onion, garlic, herbs, and spices. I usually add sunflower and pumpkin seeds to the dough for added nutrition, and sometimes a handful of grated cheddar cheese just for fun and a bit of extra flavor.

Place the flours, salt, oil or Ghee in a large mixing bowl and rub the ingredients together by hand to blend well. Stir in the water with a wooden spoon, or by hand, adding a little more if necessary to form a sticky ball. With well-floured hands, knead the dough in the bowl, or on a flat lightly floured table for 10 minutes, or until it is soft and can be slightly stretched without breaking. Cover and allow the dough to rest for 20–30 minutes. Toss the seeds together in a small bowl and set aside.

Preheat oven to 450 degrees F.

To make the crackers, you will need a flat baking sheet, or you can use the reverse side of one with a lip, to roll the dough onto. Lightly grease the baking sheet with olive oil or Ghee. Divide the dough into 4 equal pieces and cover with a damp towel. Take one piece at a time and flatten it into a 5–6-inch round disk with your hands. Generously coat both sides of the disk with the seed mixture, place on the baking sheet, and roll into thin free-form rounds about 1/4-inch thick, pressing the seeds into the dough as you go. Use a pizza wheel, dough scraper, or knife to score into squares, wedges, or whatever shape you want your crackers to be, but do not separate the pieces. Bake the crackers on the top rack of the oven for 7–10 minutes, or until they begin to brown. Remove from the oven and cool on wire racks before snapping the pieces apart. Store in an airtight container for 7–10 days..

Sourdough Starter

MAKES ABOUT 3 QUARTS

8 cups rye or wheat flour, divided

2 cups non-chlorinated water

The ancient method of natural sourdough leavening for bread is the easiest way for our bodies to digest grains. In order to make bread this way, you must have a sourdough starter. Most of the bakers in my community share their sourdough starters freely, and for the best flavor, prefer them made with rye; however, wheat flour will also work fine in this recipe.

If you are not planning on using your starter within the week, store it loosely sealed in a jar in the refrigerator. After another week or so, remove the sleepy starter from the refrigerator, pour it into a clean bowl, and blend in a little flour and water for it to eat. Remove 1 cup starter, return it to the refrigerator, and repeat the process each week until you use it again.

In a gallon-size glass jar or ceramic bowl, mix 2 cups of the flour, reserving the rest for feeding throughout the week, and the water into a paste-like consistency. Cover the top with a clean cloth, secure with a rubber band, and place the starter in a warm place. After 24 hours, and again each day for 6 more days, transfer the starter to a clean bowl, leaving any scummy stuff in the old bowl. Add 1 cup flour and 1 cup of fresh water to the mixture and blend well. Clean the bowl you used before and pour in the starter, cover with the cloth and set aside in a warm place to continue the fermentation process.

After 1 week, the starter is ready for making bread. Before making a batch of bread, reserve 1 cup to 1 quart of the starter in a clean jar or bowl, and feed it 1 cup each of flour and water once a day, to keep it alive and growing for the next use. Sourdough starter can also be stored in the refrigerator, which slows the growth of the culture, and needs to be fed just once a week. When you want to make bread, bring the starter to room temperature and feed it 1 cup flour and 1 cup water each day until you have enough volume for your recipe. Reserve 1 cup for the next batch and begin the process over again, or store your starter in the refrigerator. If you are not baking regularly you still must feed and ferment your starter. Every week or so, either use or throw away half of the starter. Pour the remainder into a clean jar, add a few tablespoons of flour and water, stir to blend, cover, and put back in the refrigerator.

NOTE: *Sourdough starter can be made into fantastic Sourdough Buckwheat Pancakes (page 41) for a deliciously different whole-grain breakfast and also incorporated into crackers, muffins, and other baked goods for additional flavor and a nice tang.*

Traditional Whole Grain Sourdough Bread

MAKES 2 LOAVES

3 cups Sourdough Starter
(page 157)

2 cups water

Approximately 8 cups whole
wheat or spelt flour (flours
hydrate differently, use more
or less accordingly, hard
winter wheat is best)

2 teaspoons sea salt

**BREAD EMBELLISHMENTS:
(GENTLY KNEAD INTO THE DOUGH
BEFORE SHAPING INTO LOAVES)**

Soaked or sprouted whole
grains: rye, wheat, oat groat,
barley, buckwheat, spelt, (see
sprouting chart page 67)

Soaked or sprouted seeds:
sunflower, pumpkins,
sesame, flax, (see sprouting
chart page 67)

Dried fruit: figs, dates,
raisins, apricots

Kalamata olives or sun-
dried tomatoes

Herbs and spices of choice

Homemade whole grain bread costs a fraction of bread purchased at the grocery store and is one of the simplest ways to save dollars on your food bill. Whole grain sourdough bread made with freshly ground flour is in a class by itself. If you have a hand or electric-powered mill, or a Vita-Mix (see glossary), to grind whole grains into flour at home, by all means use it for this recipe.

The rising time for this recipe is not as critical as for bread made with commercial yeast, and these naturally fermented loaves can take 6 hours, or more to rise, depending on the grind of flour you use and temperature of the environment. For the best texture, freshly baked loaves need to be thoroughly cooled before cutting.

Have all of the ingredients at room temperature before beginning. In a large bowl with a wooden spoon, combine the starter and water. Stir in 3 cups of the flour, 1 cup at a time, until evenly blended. Beat the batter 150 times with a wooden spoon to incorporate air and help develop the gluten in the flour. At this point, the mixture is called a sponge. Cover the bowl with a damp cloth and set it in a warm place for 3–5 hours to rise. Alternately, you can put the sponge in a cool place overnight. The longer it sits, the more sour the bread.

When the dough has doubled in volume, add 2 cups flour and sprinkle with the salt. Fold, don't stir, the flour into the dough. Continue adding the remaining flour until you have a shaggy mass and turn it out onto a flour-dusted surface. With well-floured hands, knead the dough, adding a little more flour as needed, for at least 10 minutes, or until you have a smooth and silky ball. The longer you knead, the lighter the loaf. You can use a bread machine, or the dough hook attachment on a mixer, but I prefer to knead my bread by hand and feel the transformation as I work the dough.

A dough scraper or big rubber spatula without a handle are useful tools for scraping dough off the table as you knead and are also helpful for cleaning off the work surface when done. Kneading can be a very satisfying task, and it definitely takes some effort, so do it on a surface that is at a comfortable height and get a nice rhythm going. Relax, take your time, put some muscle into your kneading, and your reward will be beautiful bread. The dough is done when it has a nice sheen and you can press it with your finger and the indentation remains.

Press the kneaded dough into a ball, place it in a generously oiled large bowl, preferably made of heavy ceramic, and roll it around to coat the surface with oil. Cover the bowl with a damp cloth and put it in a warm place to rise for 4–5 hours, or longer, depending on the temperature, or until double in bulk.

When you're ready to shape the loaves, punch down the dough and fold the edges into the center, pressing it into a ball. Turn the mass out onto a lightly floured surface, knead a few times and let rest 5 minutes before shaping. Divide the dough in half and, one at a time, press the balls into an oblong disk and roll it up lengthwise into a loaf shape. Pinch the edges together and place the dough, seam side down, into a greased bread pan, preferably made from glass or ceramic. Cut a few small diagonal slits in the top, so the steam can escape while baking. Cover the loaves with a clean cloth and place in a warm draft-free place to rise for 2–3 hours, or until double in bulk. This step can also be done overnight in a cooler environment with good results. Proofing bread with wild yeast takes longer than it does when using commercial yeast, so be patient.

When the loaves have risen, put them in a 350-degree F oven and bake for about 1 hour, or until done. Test by thumping the tops with your fingers and listening for the hollow sound that lets you know they are cooked in the middle, or the internal temperature registers 190 degrees F with a kitchen thermometer. Remove the pans from the oven, turn the hot loaves onto a wire rack and cover with a clean towel. For the best textured loaf, cool completely before cutting. Sourdough bread is naturally resistant to spoilage and these hearty loaves will keep for a week or more without refrigeration when wrapped in a paper bag or cotton cloth and kept in a cool place. They can also be stored in the refrigerator in an airtight container, or plastic bag, or double wrapped and frozen for use later.

Sourdough Rye Bread

MAKES 2 LOAVES

....

3 cups Sourdough Starter
   (page 157)

2 cups water

5 cups rye flour, more or less,
   depending on the grind

1 teaspoon sea salt

1 cup sunflower seeds, soaked*

1 cup pumpkin seeds, soaked*

*The seeds must be soaked
   overnight or at least 4 hours
   before proceeding. Have all
   of the ingredients at room
   temperature before beginning

OPTIONAL ADDITIONS:

Soaked or sprouted grains:
   rye, wheat, oat groat, barley,
   buckwheat, spelt, quinoa, wild
   rice (see sprouting chart page 67)

Soaked or sprouted seeds:
   sunflower, pumpkin, sesame, flax,
   caraway, coriander, fennel, cumin
   (see sprouting chart page 67)

Rehydrated dried fruit: figs,
   dates, raisins, apricots,
   apples or fruit of choice

Whole soaked nuts: almonds,
   pecans, cashews, walnuts,
   hazelnuts, pistachios,
   pine, or macadamia

This basic rye bread recipe is wonderful just as is, but it can be taken up a notch in flavor, nutrition, and texture with the addition of sprouted grains, seeds, dried fruit, and other ingredients. Try replacing some or all of the water with milk, buttermilk, or yogurt for more protein and tang. This bread can be put together in just minutes, making it a perfect recipe for novice bakers to get a feel for working wild sourdough into a delicious staff of life staple.

In a large bowl, preferably made from stainless steel, glass, or ceramic, stir together the starter and water. Add the flour and salt and mix well. All flour is ground differently and depending on the coarseness of the grain, you might need to add a little more flour or water to the mixture. The consistency should look like a thick muffin batter, but not as stiff as cookie dough. Add the soaked seeds, or any other additions, and mix evenly into the batter. Divide into two greased loaf pans, preferably made from glass or ceramic and smooth the tops with a rubber spatula. Cover the loaves with a piece of parchment paper and a clean dry cloth and put in a warm place to rise for at least 4 hours, or until they reach the top of the pan. The parchment paper may stick to the top of the risen loaf. If this happens, just carefully peel it off and lightly spray with a little water.

Preheat the oven to 300 degrees F.

Place the loaves in oven and bake for 1½–2 hours, or until done. Test by thumping the tops with your fingers and listening for the hollow sound that lets you know the dough is cooked in the center of the loaf. If you're not sure, the internal temperature should read 210 degrees F when tested with a kitchen thermometer. Remove the pans from the oven and cool briefly. Turn the hot loaves onto a wire rack, cover with a clean towel, and cool completely before cutting. Sourdough bread is naturally resistant to spoilage and will keep for a week, or more, without refrigeration when wrapped in a paper bag or cotton cloth. Bread stored in plastic must be refrigerated or put in a cool larder to prevent mold, and is best eaten within a few days.

Sourdough English Muffins

MAKES 12–15 MUFFINS

3 cups scalded milk, cooled

1 cup Sourdough Starter (page 157)

4 cups whole wheat or spelt bread flour (hard winter wheat is best)

2 tablespoons honey

$1/2$ cup lukewarm water

$2^1/4$ teaspoons baker's yeast or 1 packet active-dry

4 cups unbleached white flour

1 teaspoon sea salt

$1/3$ cup or more cornmeal

This recipe makes a moist, flavorful, and wholesome English muffin, the perfect foundation for Amphora Eggs Benedict (page 46). The flavor of these handcrafted muffins is well worth the effort for my loved ones and they taste so much better than the store-bought varieties.

Cooking the muffins on a hot griddle is perfect if you don't have an oven available, and it also helps the bread develop the characteristic crumbly texture we associate with traditional English muffins.

The night before you want to make these muffins, mix the milk, starter, and whole wheat flour in a bowl; cover and set aside to bloom into a frothy sponge.

In the morning, combine the honey and water in a large bread bowl, add the yeast, and set aside for 5 minutes to activate. Stir in the starter mixture made the night before and beat briskly with a wooden spoon or whisk. Mix in the unbleached white flour and the salt and turn the dough out onto a floured surface. With well-floured hands, knead the dough for 10–15 minutes, adding just a little more flour as needed, until smooth and elastic.

Sprinkle a little cornmeal on the table and roll the dough $1/2$ inch thick—this step is best done in two batches. With a cookie cutter, glass, or the top of a wide-mouth mason jar, cut the dough into circles and place them 1 inch apart on a cornmeal-sprinkled baking sheet. Do not twist the cutter or jar as you cut the rounds to ensure a full second rising of the muffins. Cover with a clean cloth.

Set the baking sheet in a warm place to rise for 1–2 hours, depending on the temperature, or until double in bulk. When the muffins have risen, place them an inch apart on a medium hot griddle and cook for 5–6 minutes, or until they begin to brown. Flip them over and continue cooking for another 4–5 minutes, or until both sides are lightly browned. Continue to flip the muffins back and forth between sides until they are done. This will keep the outside from getting too dark before the center is completely cooked. Eat hot off the grill with unsalted butter, or split and toast for a crunchy texture. Store in an airtight container and eat within several days.

Grill Bread

MAKES 4–6 SERVINGS

1 recipe Sourdough English Muffin (page 162), Pizza Dough (page 108), or other basic bread dough

Flavor accents for grill bread:

- Fresh chopped herbs: sage, rosemary, thyme, oregano, basil, chives, dill, parsley, and cilantro

- Spices: cumin, anise, coriander, chili, fennel, mustard, pepper, and paprika

- Garlic, onions, sun-dried tomatoes, and olives

Cornmeal

Grill bread is a very simple and wonderful way to make flavorful fresh bread without an oven. Many kinds of different bread dough can be used with this technique, and like pizza, grill breads don't need a long rise, making it perfect for adding a special note to last-minute meals with fresh hot bread. Experiment with different additions and combinations of flavors and create you own signature grill bread to share it with friends and family at your next special gathering—inviting and inspiring others to join you in the fun and satisfaction of making fresh delicious hand-crafted bread.

Begin with one of the recipes above, or your favorite bread dough, for the foundation of this recipe and take the dough through the first rise as instructed.

After punching down, knead in one or a combination of several of the flavor accents. On a flat surface sprinkled with a little cornmeal, take a fist-size piece of dough, roll it in a ball, and press into a 3–5-inch disk. Lightly sprinkle the dough with cornmeal and roll it out into a $1/4$–$1/2$-inch-thick free-form shape. Place the bread on a medium hot griddle, or over the coals right on the barbecue grill, and cook for 4–6 minutes, depending on the heat. Carefully turn the bread over and cook the other side until browned. Flip the bread over and move it around the heat to keep the outside from getting too dark while the inside cooks. Remove from the grill when the center is done and the bread is golden brown. Serve hot, or wrap in a towel-lined basket to keep warm.

Honey Whole Grain Bread

MAKES 2 LOAVES

....

3 cups lukewarm water

1/3 cup honey

1 tablespoon dry baker's yeast
   or 1 package active-dry

6 to 8 cups whole wheat or spelt
   flour, more or less, depending
   on the grind of the flour

1/3 cup rolled oats

1/4 cup millet

1/4 cup corn flour

1/4 cup rye flour

2 tablespoons vital wheat
   gluten, optional

1/4 cup vegetable oil, optional

1 tablespoon sea salt

This honest loaf of wholesome bread is made with commercial baker's yeast instead of the wild starter used in sourdough breads. It slices well, making it a good choice for sandwiches, and, when toasted, the sweetness of the whole grains blooms. If you like, add vital wheat gluten or substitute up to half of the whole wheat flour with unbleached white for a lighter loaf; however, this will lessen the nutritional value accordingly.

In a large mixing bowl, combine the water and honey and then sprinkle in the yeast and stir into the liquid. Set the bowl aside for 5 minutes to be sure the yeast blooms.

Add 3 cups whole wheat flour to the bowl in 1/2-cup increments, beating well after each addition. With a wooden spoon or wire whisk, vigorously beat the batter 100 times until the batter has a smooth and stretchy consistency. Stir in the oats, millet, and corn and rye flours, add the vital wheat gluten, if using, and beat another 50 times to incorporate. Cover the bowl with a damp towel and set it in a warm place to rise for about 1 hour, or until the sponge doubles in size.

Pour the oil, if using, around the sides of the bowl and sprinkle the dough with the salt. With a dough scraper, or rubber spatula, fold, do not stir the sides of the dough towards the center as you spin the bowl around. Sprinkle in the remaining whole wheat flour in 1/2-cup increments and mix with a wooden spoon or hands until it forms a shaggy ball and the dough begins to hang together. Turn the dough, and scattered pieces, onto a floured surface and press it into a ball. With well-floured hands, knead the dough, adding a little more flour as necessary, for at least 10 minutes, or until you have a smooth and silky ball.

The longer you knead, the lighter the loaf. You can use a bread machine, or the dough hook attachment on a mixer, but I prefer to knead my bread by hand and feel the transformation as I work the dough. Kneading can be a very satisfying task, and it takes some effort. Do the work on a surface that is at a comfortable height for you to get a nice rhythm going. Relax, take your time, put a little muscle into your kneading, and your reward will be beautiful bread. When the dough is done it will have a nice sheen, and when pressed with your finger, the indentation remains.

Press the kneaded dough into a ball, place it in a generously oiled large bowl, preferably made of heavy ceramic, and roll it around to coat the surface with oil. Cover and set in a warm place to rise for an hour or until it doubles in size. Punch down the dough, cover, and let it rise for another hour, or until doubled in volume. Allowing the dough to rise a second time gives you a lighter loaf in exchange for the extra time. Punch down the dough again and divide it into 2 pieces. Roll each one into a ball, spinning the dough around with one hand as you go, and roll it into a log shape that will fit nicely into your bread pan. Pinch the seam together and place in a greased bread pan with the seam side down. Gently flatten the dough into the corners of the pan, cover, and set in a warm place to rise for 45 minutes–1 hour, or until it has risen to the top of the pan.

Preheat the oven to 350 degrees F.

Make a few small slits in the top for the steam to escape and spray with a little water to soften the crust. Place the loaves in the oven and bake for about 1 hour, or until done. Test by thumping the tops with your fingers and listening for the hollow sound that lets you know they are cooked in the middle, or the internal temperature registers 185 degrees F with a kitchen thermometer. Remove the pans from the oven and turn the hot loaves onto a wire rack. Cover with a clean towel and cool completely before cutting for the best textured loaf. Fresh bread is always best when eaten within a few days and should be stored in a cool place wrapped in cloth or a paper bag. If you store bread in the refrigerator, put it in an airtight container or plastic bag, and if you want to freeze a loaf for use later on, double wrap it to prevent freezer burn.

Whole Grain Scones

1¼ cups whole wheat or
    spelt pastry flour

¼ cup corn flour

1 tablespoon baking powder

½ teaspoon baking soda

½ teaspoon sea salt

½ cup rolled oats

6 tablespoons unsalted butter

1 cup buttermilk

Scones can be embellished
with a variety of sweet and savory
additions to complement whatever
else you're serving; incorporate cut
pieces of dried or fresh fruit, jam
or preserves, and chocolate chips,
nuts, seeds, fresh chopped herbs,
spices, grated cheese, or whatever
sounds good to you in a scone. For
the best texture, combine additions
with the dry ingredients before
adding the buttermilk.

Scones are free-formed biscuits that can easily incorporate a
wide variety of whole grain flours and can be made either sweet
or savory to complement whatever else is being served. Cream,
half-and-half, milk, or yogurt can replace or be combined with
the buttermilk in this recipe. Each addition or substitution will
have a slightly different texture, but will still produce a richly
flavored and crumbly scone. If you're a vegan, this recipe can also
be made with coconut or olive oil and non-dairy milk with good
results. For the best texture, it is important to mix the wet and dry
ingredients quickly and refrain from handling the dough too much
before baking. Scones are very forgiving, and with the proper
ratio of wet to dry ingredients, even a beginning cook can create
signature scones with ease.

Preheat the oven to 425 degrees F.

Sift together the flours, baking powder, baking soda, and salt into a
food processor with the S-blade attachment, or large mixing bowl.
Add the oats and stir to combine. Cut the butter into the flour mixture
with pulses in the food processor, or by hand with a pastry cutter and
quick hands. Place the flour mixture into a large bowl, create a well in
the center, add the buttermilk, and combine with a few swift strokes.
Roll the dough onto a lightly floured surface and gently pat it into an
8-inch round, about ¾ inch thick. Place the disk on a lightly floured
or parchment paper-lined baking sheet and cut into wedges, like a
pie, gently spreading the pieces about ½ inch apart. Bake for 12–15
minutes, or until the tops begin to brown and the center is cooked.
Remove from the oven and serve while hot. Scones can be stored in an
airtight container, or refrigerated in plastic for several days.

Desserts

The Art of Pie

A freshly baked pie is at the top of my comfort-food list and with just a little bit of practice, making them is fast and easy. When I teach baking and cooking classes at Esalen, on the last morning we always make pies, and each participant takes home their own handcrafted creation to share with family and friends as a memento of our workshop and the skills they learned. Pies come in many different sizes, shapes and designs. Begin with making a simple bottom crust only recipe like an open-faced cream pie, pizza dough, or a fresh fruit tart. After you've practiced your rolling techniques, try adding a solid, lattice, or crumb topping and expand your repertoire. Minimal handling is essential for making flakey piecrusts. Using a food processor is helpful, just be careful not to pulse the ingredients too much, or the butter will melt into the flour and your crust will be tough. Of course, the old-fashioned way of using a pastry cutter or experienced hands will do, just be sure that the butter is very cold, or frozen, when you begin and work fast. This recipe can be used for savory pies by just omitting the sweetener and adding your favorite filling. Whether sweet or savory, making homemade pies is well worth the effort, and always appreciated by all who are fortunate enough to share in the fruits of your good work.

Basic Sweet Pie Dough

MAKES 2 (10-INCH) PIES

....

4¼ cups sifted whole wheat
   or spelt pastry flour

2 cups unsalted butter, cut
   into 1-inch chunks

3 tablespoons sucanat or
   granulated sweetener of choice

½ teaspoon sea salt

¾ to 1 cup ice cold water

Put the flour, butter, sucanat, and salt into a food processor and pulse until it resembles a course meal. If you use sucanat, the dough will have a speckled appearance. Do not overwork the dough or it will be tough. Slowly add the water, until the dough begins to come together, but before it gets wet and sticky. Divide the dough in half and press into balls. For the best texture, handle the dough as little as possible. With flour-dusted hands, press the center of the ball and flatten it into a 3–4-inch disk, tucking any cracks on the under-side as you go. Wrap the disks in plastic, or place in a covered bowl, and refrigerate for at least 1 hour. This will make the dough easier to handle when you roll it out.

ROLLING THE DOUGH:

Place the dough disks on a floured table or counter and begin rolling from the center out toward the sides. After several strokes, move the dough in a quarter circle to keep it from sticking to the table and continue moving and rolling until crust is approximately ⅛-inch thick and 12 inches in diameter, dusting with a little flour as you go. Place the rolling pin across the center of the circle, gently lift half of the dough, and drape it onto the pin. Place the pie plate close to the center of the dough, carefully lift, center, and roll the crust off the pin and onto the plate. Gently lift the edges of the dough so that gravity lowers it into place on the bottom, and be sure to not stretch the dough in the process.

The edges should almost be touching the table, or evenly trimmed, if needed. Roll the edge of the dough up onto the lip of the plate, it will be several layers thick, and give it a little squeeze as you spin the plate around to even out. To keep the crust from burning before the pie is fully baked, be sure to make the edging nice and plump. If you are making a single-crust, or crumb-topped pie, gently squeeze the edges together to form a nice lip of dough. Using two fingers on one side of the lip and one finger on the other, crimp to form a pretty fluted edge as you spin the pie plate around again. For double-crusted pies, or lattice pies, add filling, cover with another layer of dough, or cut and neatly weave the strips, then proceed as above with crimping and fluting the edge. Prepared pie shells can be double wrapped and frozen for later use.

Butternut Squash Pie with Maple Whipped Cream

MAKES 8–10 SERVINGS

3 cups (2-inch chunks) roasted or steamed butternut squash, cooled

1/2 cup maple syrup

1/3 cup sucanat

3 eggs

1 cup half-and-half

2 tablespoons molasses

2 teaspoons cinnamon

1 teaspoon cardamom

1/2 teaspoon gingerroot

1/2 teaspoon cloves

1/2 teaspoon nutmeg

1/4 teaspoon sea salt

1 teaspoon vanilla

1 (10-inch) unbaked pie shell, with fluted edges (page 169)

MAPLE WHIPPED CREAM

1 cup heavy cream

1/4 cup maple syrup

1/2 teaspoon vanilla

Winter squash roasted in the oven develops a deep rich flavor, and many heirloom varieties are perfect for pies. In my kitchen, butternut is the queen of them all. It has less water, seeds, and stringy stuff than most pumpkins and is used in this traditional harvest-time recipe made with maple syrup and sucanat. I love the deep flavor of roasted squash, but if you are short on time, steaming is a good option and will work fine for this recipe. Winter squash is loaded with essential nutrients, fiber, and great flavor. When combined with fresh eggs, rich half-and-half, and warming spices, a piece of this wholesome pie is practically a meal in itself.

Preheat oven to 350 degrees F.

Place the squash, maple syrup, sucanat, and eggs in a food processor and blend well. Add the half-and-half, molasses, spices, and vanilla and process until smooth and creamy. Pour the filling into the pie shell and bake for 50–60 minutes, or until set and a knife inserted in the center comes out clean. Remove from the oven, place on a wire rack, and cool completely before cutting. Serve with a dollop of Maple Whipped Cream.

MAPLE WHIPPED CREAM

To make the cream, place a medium-size stainless steel bowl in the freezer for 5 minutes to chill. Remove the bowl from the freezer, pour in the cream, and beat with an electric mixer, or by hand with a wire whisk, until it begins to thicken. Drizzle in the maple syrup and continue beating until the cream is thick and it holds a soft peak. Do not over beat or the texture will be compromised. Stir in the vanilla and serve.

To roast squash, preheat oven to 400 degrees F. Cut 2 medium-size butternut squash in half, remove the seeds and strings, and place the pieces cut side down in an ovenproof baking dish. Add 1/2 cup water and bake for 45 minutes–1 hour, or until tender. Cool, peel the squash, and cut it into chunks that will be easy for your food processor to handle.

To steam squash, cut 2 medium-size butternut squash into 2-inch chunks and steam until tender. Peel off the skin and proceed with filling recipe above.

Spicy Pear Pie

MAPLE PECAN CRUMB TOPPING

4 tablespoons unsalted butter

$1/3$ cup whole wheat pastry flour

$1/4$ cup sucanat

$1/2$ cup rolled oats

1 teaspoon cinnamon

$1/2$ cup chopped pecans

$1/4$ cup maple syrup

6 cups thinly sliced firm ripe pears

1 tablespoon fresh lemon juice

$1/2$ cup sucanat

1 to 2 tablespoons ground tapioca, depending on the juiciness of the fruit

1 teaspoon freshly grated gingerroot or $1/2$ teaspoon ground

$1/2$ teaspoon cinnamon

$1/4$ teaspoon cardamom

1 (10-inch) unbaked pie shell, with fluted edges (page 169)

As a professional, I've made hundreds of fresh fruit pies, and this is one of the most popular fall offerings from the days of the Café Amphora. The crispy ripe pears that came from the local orchards made my pies shine and I used them whenever possible. Freshly grated gingerroot and a spicy pecan crumb topping are the magic ingredients for transforming fresh firm ripe pears into a magnificent fall dessert pie, especially when topped with a big scoop of vanilla ice cream.

In a food processor or by hand, cut the butter into the flour and sucanat until crumbly. Add the oats, cinnamon, and pecans and blend into the flour mixture. Drizzle in the maple syrup and toss to combine with the topping.

Preheat oven to 400 degrees F.

Place the pears into a large mixing bowl and toss with the lemon juice. Add the sucanat, tapioca, and spices and toss again. Fill the fluted piecrust with the fruit and top with Maple Pecan Crumb Topping. Bake for 50–60 minutes or until bubbly and golden brown. Cool completely before cutting.

Fresh Summer Fruit Tart with Honey Citrus Cream

....

TART SHELL

1¹/₂ cups whole wheat pastry
  or unbleached white flour

2 tablespoons sucanat or
  granulated sweetener of choice

¹/₄ teaspoon sea salt

¹/₃ cup cold unsalted butter,
  cut into ¹/₂-inch chunks

HONEY CITRUS CREAM

4 large eggs

²/₃ cup honey

¹/₃ cup fresh lemon juice

¹/₃ cup fresh lime juice

2 teaspoons lemon zest

2 teaspoons lime zest

¹/₂ cup unsalted butter, cut
  into 1-inch pieces

1 basket fresh strawberries,
  or 2 cups

1 basket fresh raspberries, or 1 cup

1 basket fresh blueberries, or 1 cup

2 fresh kiwi, peeled and sliced
  into ¹/₄-inch circles

¹/₄ cup red current jelly

1 tablespoon lemon juice

The fusion of fresh lemon and lime makes this tart burst with citrus flavor and is a perfect bed for fresh summer fruit. Topped with colorful berries and brushed with a red currant glaze, this simple tart is a light and refreshing dessert to help you celebrate summer's sweetness with flair.

Preheat the oven to 400 degrees F.

Mix the flour, sucanat, and salt in a food processor. Add the butter and pulse until it is crumbly and the mixture begins to clump together. If you used sucanat, the dough will look speckled but taste great. Press the dough into a ball and let rest for 10 minutes to fully hydrate the grains. Using your knuckle, fingers, thumb, and palm, press the dough evenly to about ¹/₄-inch thickness in the bottom and up the sides of an 11–12-inch tart pan with a removable rim. Prick the bottom using a fork in several places and bake for 15–20 minutes, or until the crust begins to brown. Cool completely before filling.

In a small bowl, whisk the eggs and honey together until light and fluffy. In a double boiler, combine the egg and honey mixture, the juices, and zests and cook, stirring constantly, until thick. Remove from heat and stir in the butter until smooth and silky. Cool the citrus cream completely, stirring several times to prevent a "skin" from forming on the top. Cover and refrigerate for at least 1 hour before serving, or store in a sealed jar in the refrigerator for up to 1 week.

ASSEMBLING THE TART:

With a spatula, spread the cream evenly on the tart crust. Beginning at the outside rim, carefully place the fruit in a decorative mandala pattern, overlapping as you go to make it pretty. Begin with the biggest of the strawberries and cut them in half, leaving the green stems on if they are fresh and beautiful, and place them stem side out around the edge. If the greens are not looking pretty, core them off and place the tips of the strawberry at the outer edge. Stem and slice the remaining strawberries in half and shingle in layers, balancing the sizes as you go around in concentric circles. Integrate the raspberries, blueberries, and kiwi as you work towards the center of the tart, ending with a big beautiful strawberry, or mound of berries.

Combine the red currant jelly and lemon juice in a small saucepan. Heat, stirring constantly, until the jelly has melted. Remove from the heat and, with a pastry brush, carefully glaze the tops of the fruit.

Creamy Options

For special occasions in our family, we often make Honey Citrus Cream with the addition of orange, tangerine, or grapefruit juice and zest, using whatever combination of citrus is in season. Each person is given a little dish of the rich glossy citrus cream, a freshly baked Golden Oatmeal Cookie (page 181), and a handful of fresh strawberries or blueberries for a heavenly whole foods treat.

Blonde Baked Tart Shell

For a 'blonde', or partially baked shell, remove from the oven after 8–10 minutes. Carefully add the filling of choice and continue baking until the center is set and the edges are golden brown.

This variation is used in the Cherry Pecan Tart recipe that follows this one, but can also be used with any of your favorite baked "custard-like" tart or pie fillings. Be creative!

Fresh Cherry Pecan Tart

MAKES 8–10 SERVINGS

FILLING

¹/₂ cup sucanat or sugar

3 tablespoons softened
  unsalted butter

¹/₄ teaspoon sea salt

2 eggs

1 egg yolk

1 cup heavy cream

¹/₂ teaspoon vanilla

1 cup ground pecans

1 blonde-baked Tart Shell
  (page 173)

3 cups pitted fresh cherries

CHOCOLATE GANACHE

¹/₂ cup heavy cream

5 ounces bitter sweet chocolate,
  chopped into chunks

1 cup Maple Whipped Cream
  (page 170), optional

This is one of the seasonal favorites developed at the Café Amphora, and with cherries being the first summer pit fruit available, everyone loved this tart. The spectacular presentation, with fresh cherries peaking out of a creamy pecan filling and drizzled with chocolate, would seduce customers into following our posted motto: "Life is uncertain, eat dessert first!" You can use any variety of fresh cherry for this recipe, but they must be very fresh and firm. To remove the pit, an inexpensive hand pitter works best and keeps the cherry whole, but a paring knife will work if you are very careful. This is a deliciously rich and filling dessert that I have made with almonds, macadamia nuts, and walnuts, as well as other fruits. All are tasty, but cherries and pecans are still my first choice for this tasty tart.

Preheat oven to 350 degrees F.

Place the sucanat, butter, and salt in a large mixing bowl and beat with a wooden spoon, whisk, or electric beaters until well blended. Add the eggs and yolk and continue beating until the sucanat granules have completely blended in and the mixture is light and creamy, about 3 minutes. Stir in the cream and vanilla, add the ground nuts and mix well. Spread the filling in the tart shell and nest the cherries on top, wiggling them gently into the filling with your fingers. Bake the tart for 30–35 minutes, or until the filling is set and the top is golden brown. Cool completely on a wire rack before applying the chocolate. Score the pieces to mark each serving.

In a small saucepan over medium heat, bring the cream just up to a boil. Place the chocolate chunks in a medium-size stainless steel, glass, or ceramic mixing bowl and pour the hot cream over the pieces. Let the mixture sit, without stirring, for a couple of minutes to melt the chocolate with the residual heat. With a wire whisk, blend the chocolate and cream together until smooth and silky. Cool completely, stirring several times to prevent a skin from forming on the top before using.

Put the ganache in a pastry bag with a small round tip and drizzle a thin line back and forth from side to side of each piece, starting at the outer edge and moving towards the center of each serving. Take a knife and gently run it up the center of each piece to make an éclair-like design on each serving. Cut and serve plain, or with a dollop of Maple Whipped Cream (page 170).

Ricotta Cheesecake

....

4 eggs

4 cups ricotta cheese

$^3/_4$ cup sucanat or sugar

$^1/_3$ cup whole wheat pastry flour

2 teaspoons vanilla

1 teaspoon cinnamon

$^1/_4$ teaspoon fresh grated nutmeg

$^1/_4$ teaspoon sea salt

2 tablespoons fresh lemon juice

2 teaspoons orange zest

2 teaspoons lemon zest

This lighter version of cheesecake with an Italian slant is inspired by my fondness of fresh ricotta. This is one of my favorite desserts, made in many variations over the years, especially when the recipe is multiplied to make several hundred servings at a time!

Preheat oven to 350 degrees F.

Generously grease and flour a 10-inch spring-form pan and set it aside.

Separate the eggs into 2 separate large mixing bowls. Place the ricotta in a food processor fitted with the S-blade and process until smooth and creamy. You may need to do this step in two batches depending on the size of your machine. In the bowl with the egg yolks, add the ricotta and remaining ingredients, except for the egg whites, and beat with an electric mixer on high speed for 2 minutes, scraping the sides of the bowl as needed. When you begin, the batter will look speckled if you used sucanat but just keep mixing until the batter becomes smooth.

With an electric mixer or wire whisk, beat the egg whites until stiff, but not dry. Gently fold the whites into the cheese mixture until evenly blended. Pour the batter into the prepared pan and give it a little wiggle to even the top. Bake for about 1 hour, or until the cheesecake is set, a toothpick inserted in the center comes out clean, and the top is golden. Remove from the oven and place on a wire rack.

When the cake has cooled completely, cover and chill for several hours or overnight for before serving. To serve, carefully run a knife around the cake and remove the rim of the pan. Place it on a serving platter and for special occasions, embellish with fresh fruit slices and berries, a sauce made with fresh, or dried fruit, Luscious Chocolate Frosting (page 177), a drizzle of Chocolate Ganache (facing page), or your favorite homemade dessert topping.

Amphora Chocolate Cake

MAKES 1 (10-INCH)
BUNDT CAKE OR
3 (9-INCH) CAKE PANS

2 cups whole wheat pastry or
    unbleached white flour

2 cups sucanat or sugar

1 cup unsweetened cocoa

1 teaspoon baking powder

1$\frac{1}{2}$ teaspoons baking soda

1 teaspoon sea salt

1 cup whole milk, room temperature

3 eggs, room temperature

$\frac{1}{2}$ cup rice bran, sunflower, or
    light vegetable oil of choice

1 teaspoon vanilla

1 cup boiling water

$\frac{3}{4}$ cup homemade or natural
    store-bought raspberry
    jam (opposite page)

On any busy day at the Café Amphora, several of these luscious chocolate cakes were eaten, piece by piece, all day long. They were Bundt cakes filled with raspberry jam, as well as other surprise fillings, and then slathered with big waves of silky chocolate frosting. It was a chocolate lover's dream cake! Back in those days, I made this cake with white sugar and white flour. However, today I prefer to make this recipe with sucanat, an unrefined sweetener that was not even available back then, and whole wheat pastry flour instead of white. This is one of those recipes that unrefined sweeteners and whole grains can be integrated into without compromising the texture and flavor. To be true to tradition, it can be made both ways and the choice is yours. Either way you choose, this chocolate cake is a winner.

Preheat oven to 350 degrees F.

In a large mixing bowl, sift together the flour, sucanat or sugar, cocoa, baking powder, baking soda, and salt.

In a small mixing bowl, whisk together the milk, eggs, oil, and vanilla. Combine the wet and dry ingredients and beat with an electric mixer for 2 minutes on high, scraping the sides of the bowl as you go, or whisk vigorously for 3–4 minutes by hand. Stir in the boiling water and blend well. Pour the batter into a greased and floured Bundt pan and bake for 50–55 minutes, or until done. Check by inserting a toothpick in the center—if it comes out clean, the cake is done. Remove the pan from the oven, place on a wire rack and let sit for 10–15 minutes. To remove, carefully run a knife around the sides and middle of the cake and turn it onto the wire rack. Cool before frosting.

While the cake is baking, prepare the frosting recipe on opposite page. When the cake is completely cool, line up two toothpicks on one side of the cake, with one towards the bottom and one towards the top, and begin your cut between them. This will help you line up the layers after filling the middle, just in case your cut is a bit uneven. With a serrated knife, carefully cut the cake in half horizontally as you go around, Remove the top layer, spread the jam on the bottom layer, and cover with $\frac{1}{2}$ cup of the frosting. Replace the top layer and spread the top, side, and middle of the cake with the remaining frosting.

LUSCIOUS CHOCOLATE FROSTING

1¼ cups heavy whipping cream

1¼ cups sucanat or sugar

5 ounces unsweetened Baker's Chocolate (5 squares), cut into 1-inch chunks

½ cup unsalted butter, cut into 1-inch chunks

1 teaspoon vanilla

In a heavy-bottom saucepan, combine the cream and sucanat, or sugar, and slowly bring to a boil, stirring constantly to ensure a silky finish. Lower the heat, stop stirring, and keep the mixture going at a low rolling boil for 6 minutes, watching carefully that it doesn't boil over. Place the chunks of chocolate and butter into a stainless steel or glass mixing bowl. Remove the cream from the heat, pour it over the chocolate and butter, and let it sit for a few minutes to thoroughly melt the chocolate with the residual heat. Add the vanilla and whisk the cream and chocolate mixtures together, scraping the sides of the bowl with a spatula, until smooth and silky. Cool completely, stirring several times to release the heat, before frosting the cake.

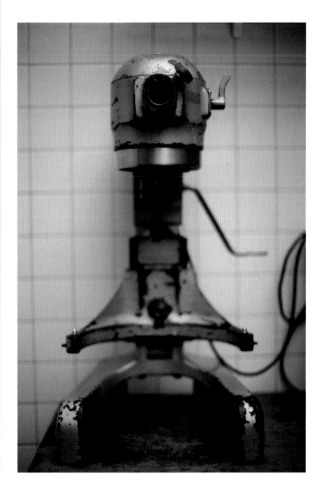

Quick Fresh Raspberry Jam

- 1½ cups fresh raspberries
- ¼ cup agave nectar or sweetener of choice
- 1 to 2 teaspoons fresh lemon juice, or to taste

Combine raspberries and agave nectar in a small heavy-bottom saucepan and gently heat until it begins to simmer. Reduce heat and continue simmering until mixture thickens and the berries begin to fall apart, 15–20 minutes. To prevent scorching, stir occasionally. Remove saucepan from the heat and stir in lemon juice, to taste. Jam will thicken as it cools.

Apple-Raspberry Crisp

TOPPING

1/2 cup unsalted butter, cut
   into 1/2-inch pieces

1 cup sucanat or brown sugar

1/2 cup whole wheat pastry flour

1 cup rolled oats

1 tablespoon cinnamon, optional

8 cups sliced firm apples (8 to 10
   whole apples or 2 to 3 pounds)

1 tablespoon fresh lemon juice

2 tablespoons whole wheat pastry
   flour or tapioca powder

4 cups fresh raspberries

Fresh seasonal fruit topped with a luscious crumb crust still warm from the oven and a dollop of vanilla ice cream melting slowly over the edges is one of my favorite desserts. Firm-fleshed apples, like Pippin or Granny Smith, have good flavor and will hold their shape better than softer textured varieties. I love to use the many heirloom varieties available at the farmers market, beginning with the early apples in late summer and the others that ripen throughout the fall harvest. Raspberries are one of the premier summer fruits, and usually last until the early apples arrive when I weave them into this yummy bright red treat.
As the seasons change, substitute the apples and raspberries with pears, peaches, nectarines, apricots, plums, rhubarb, figs, persimmons, kiwi, blueberries, strawberries, blackberries, or tropical fruits, adding a little flour, or more sweetener, depending on the juiciness and tartness of the fruit you're using.

Place the butter, sucanat, and flour in a food processor and pulse until crumbly. Add the oats and cinnamon, if using, and pulse again. By hand, use a pastry cutter or your fingertips to cut the butter into the sweetener and grains until evenly blended, but still crumbly. Set aside until ready to use.

Preheat oven to 375 degrees F.

In a large bowl, toss the apples with the lemon juice. Sprinkle in the flour, add the raspberries, and gently toss. Place the fruit in an 8 x 12-inch ovenproof glass or ceramic baking dish and evenly distribute the crumb topping to cover the top. Put your hand on the side of the dish as you sprinkle and gently press the topping around the edges to hold in place. Bake for 40–50 minutes, or until the fruit is tender and the topping is nicely browned.

Golden Oatmeal Cookies

MAKES 4 DOZEN COOKIES

$1^1/_2$ cups sucanat

$^1/_2$ cup barley malt

1 cup unsalted butter, at room temperature

2 eggs

$^1/_4$ teaspoon orange zest

1 teaspoon vanilla

$^1/_2$ teaspoon sea salt

$^1/_2$ teaspoon baking soda

2 cups whole wheat or spelt pastry flour

2 cups rolled oats

1 cup unsweetened shredded coconut

1 cup golden raisins

1 cup chopped pecans or walnuts

These cookies are made without white flour or white sugar, but you won't miss them at all. Sucanat, barley malt, coconut, and raisins are whole food sweeteners that make for a delicious and satisfying cookie that tastes just like mama made, but only better for you. I love giving a batch of these tasty cookies to friends and family who tend to shun health foods, and watch them happily eat their words.

Preheat oven to 350 degrees F.

In a large mixing bowl, blend the sucanat, barley malt, and butter. Beat the eggs in a separate bowl with the orange zest and vanilla; add to the butter mixture and mix in well. In a separate bowl, stir the salt and baking soda into the flour then mix with the wet ingredients until thoroughly combined. Add the oats, coconut, raisins, and pecans and mix into the batter until evenly distributed. On a greased or parchment paper-lined baking sheet, drop 1 rounded tablespoon of dough per cookie about 1 inch apart and bake for 10–12 minutes, or until golden brown. Cool on a wire rack and store in an airtight container for up to 1 week.

Date Nut Bars

MAKES 12 BARS

1 cup (¹/₂-inch pieces) dates, about 10 to 12 large pitted Medjools

¹/₄ to ¹/₃ cup water, depending on variety and density of dates

1 teaspoon lemon zest

²/₃ cup rolled oats

²/₃ cup whole wheat pastry flour

²/₃ cup sucanat

¹/₂ teaspoon sea salt

1 teaspoon cinnamon

¹/₄ teaspoon cardamom

1¹/₃ cups butter

1 cup pecan halves or pieces

Date bars are a wholesome easy-to-make treat that moms can feel good about giving to their kids when they ask for something sweet. Dates are high in tryptophan, an amino acid that can have a calming effect on children, and adults, too. Figs, raisins, or Dried Fruit Compote (page 38) can replace the dates in these delicious bars for a wholesome treat that is sure to satisfy a sweet tooth

Heat oven to 350 degrees F.

Place dates, water, and lemon zest in small saucepan, cover and simmer for 10 minutes or until dates are soft; remove from the heat and cool.

Place the oats in a food processor and process into coarse-grained flour. Add the whole wheat pastry flour, sucanat, salt, cinnamon, and cardamom and process again briefly. Cut the butter into the bowl and pulse to incorporate evenly into the dry ingredients, stopping as the dough begins to clump. Grease an 8 x 8-inch straight-side baking dish with a little butter and press half of the dough onto the bottom. Spread the cooked dates evenly across the top and cover with pecans. Sprinkle the remaining dough evenly over all and gently press the topping into place. Bake for 25–30 minutes, or until the top begins to brown. When done, set the baking dish on a wire rack to cool. To avoid crumbling bars, cool completely before cutting. Wrap individually to keep fresh for lunches, snacks, and kids on the go. Store in an airtight container in the refrigerator for up to 5 days.

Yam Candy

....

6 cups ($^3/_4$-inch chunks) yams

2 tablespoons melted coconut
  oil or Ghee (page 150)

$^1/_4$ teaspoon sea salt

$^1/_4$ cup maple syrup

When the kids ask for sweets, yam candy is a simple treat that parents can feel good about, and this recipe is so easy they can make these tasty morsels all by themselves. Yams are full of fiber, vitamins C and B6, potassium, and beta-carotene, and have a lower glycemic index than white potatoes. This recipe can be put together quickly and is one of my favorite ways of preparing these glorious tubers. You can use any yam or hard winter squash for this recipe, but Garnett yams have the very best flavor and the creamiest texture of all.

Preheat oven to 400 degrees F.

In a large mixing bowl, toss the yams, oil, salt, and syrup until all the pieces are evenly coated. Spread the yams on a parchment paper-lined baking sheet, without crowding the pieces, and bake for 30 minutes, or until all the pieces are soft and the edges begin to brown. Using a spatula, carefully toss the yams once or twice while they bake. When the thickest parts are completely soft, remove from the oven and cool, leaving the pieces on the tray. Yam candy does not require refrigeration for a day or two, but can be stored in an airtight container in the refrigerator for up to 1 week.

Bliss Balls

MAKES ABOUT 50 BALLS

2 cups organic whole almonds,
   raw or lightly toasted

2 cups organic dried fruit or fruit
   of choice cut into 1-inch pieces

1½ cups organic dried unsweetened
   coconut flakes, divided

¼ cup honey or agave nectar

1 teaspoon ground cinnamon

¼ teaspoon ground allspice
   or cardamom

½ teaspoon fresh grated nutmeg

½ teaspoon orange zest

½ teaspoon lemon or lime zest

Bliss balls are a nut, fruit, and spice candy—a special treat my children grew up with that is still a family favorite today. These tasty morsels can be made with a variety of nuts, seeds, dried fruit, and embellished with cocoa, spices, and other wonderful flavors for a healthy alternative to sugary desserts.

Leave the almonds raw, or lightly toast in a 300-degree F oven for 8–10 minutes. Note that the oil will continue to cook the nuts even after they come out of the oven, so be careful not to over roast them or they can become bitter. If you're using toasted nuts, cool them completely before the next step. Place the almonds in a food processor and process into a fine meal. Add the dried fruit and 1 cup coconut and process until well blended, scraping the sides of the bowl as you go.

In a separate bowl, combine the honey, spices, and zests, add to the mixture, and blend to combine. Pinch off about a teaspoon-size piece and roll it with your hands into a ball. Place the remaining coconut in a shallow bowl and add the balls, one at a time, rolling them around to coat evenly. Store in an airtight container in the refrigerator for up to 2 weeks.

Glossary

AGAR-AGAR: A clear, flavorless sea vegetable that has been freeze-dried and made into sticks, flakes, or powder and is used mainly as a thickener and substitute for gelatin.

AGAVE NECTAR: Sweet syrup made from the nectar found at the heart of the agave plant. A natural sweetener that is slowly absorbed into the body, and, like honey, it is sweeter than refined sugar, so you need less. Agave is the lowest sweetener on the glycemic index and can often be tolerated by people with sensitivities to sugar.

BARLEY MALT: A natural sweetener made from sprouted barley that has a rich nutty flavor, and is what makes malted milk shakes so wonderful.

BEE POLLEN: An amazing super food collected from honey bees that contains all the essential amino acids, as well as high amounts of vitamins, minerals, and enzymes. Bee pollen has numerous health-giving properties, especially for building a strong immune system.

BOUQUET GARNI: A bundle of herbs consisting of a bay leaf, peppercorns, parsley, thyme, and any other seasonal herb you want to incorporate, depending on the dish you're making. With the fresh herbs still on the stem, the bouquet garni is tied together with string, or wrapped into a 6-inch square of cheesecloth. It is then put into stocks, soups and stews to infuse herbal flavor and then discarded before serving.

BRAGG'S LIQUID AMINOS: A liquid seasoning that tastes similar to tamari and adds flavor to soups, sauces, and dressings. Use sparingly, as it has a strong flavor that can be overbearing if used in excess.

CACAO: A fermented and ground whole bean that is used to make chocolate. The cocoa powder found in supermarkets has been roasted. Raw cacao powder can be found in natural food stores or online.

CAROB: A Mediterranean legume that is ground into a powder and often used as a caffeine-free substitute for chocolate.

CHERIMOYA: A knobby-skinned, green-colored exotic fruit filled with a lot of large black seeds and creamy white flesh. When ripe, it will yield to slight pressure much like an avocado, and can be stored in the refrigerator for several days. The flesh tastes like a blend of mango, pineapple, and strawberry, and is the only edible part of the fruit.

CHIFFONADE: A technique for cutting basil and other tender greens into very thin strips. The leaves are rolled lengthwise, like a cigar, and then cut very thinly from tip to stem, forming thin ribbon-like pieces.

CHIPOTLE PEPPERS: A smoked jalapeño pepper that is either dry or canned in adobe sauce, and is a very flavorful condiment for adding a smoky spice to soups, sauces, beans, and other savory south-of-the-border dishes.

CLAY COOKERS: A cooking vessel made of unglazed clay that is used in many forms throughout the world. The top and bottom pieces are soaked in water before use, which creates a moist enclosed environment that steams the food, making it healthier, moister, and more flavorful than conventional methods.

COMMUNITY SUPPORTED AGRICULTURE (CSA): A sustainable system of producing and distributing fresh wholesome foods by connecting local farmers with local consumers. Based on a mutual commitment, the farmer receives an annual fee from each member and in return they receive a weekly box of fresh produce and other farm fresh foods throughout the growing season.

COTIJA CHEESE: A dry and firm Mexican cheese with a flavor that is a cross between mild Parmesan and Greek Feta. Cotija doesn't melt very well and is usually crumbled or grated as a topping for tacos, tostadas, soups, salads, beans, and other savory dishes.

DASHI: A combination of dried seaweed and small fish flakes that is a main ingredient of traditional miso soup. Dashi can be found in oriental markets and specialty stores.

FLAX SEEDS: A rich source of essential fatty acids, vitamins, and minerals. Flax seeds are 30 percent oil, and freshly grinding them for each use is the best way to unleash the numerous healthful properties of this little nutritional gem.

FEIJOA: Also know as pineapple guava, the feijoa is an egg-shaped fruit that has a sweet seedy pulp and tropical aroma. They add a tropical taste to fruit salads and smoothies and are also high in vitamin C.

FISH SAUCE: A condiment made from fermented fish that is a popular flavoring staple ingredient of Southeast Asian cuisine, especially in Thai dishes. This rich and salty sauce can be found in Oriental markets or the specialty section of many grocery stores.

GOJI BERRY: A small, red-colored dried fruit, also known as wolfberry. Goji berries have been used for centuries in traditional Chinese medicine for their nutritional and antioxidant properties. Look for them in natural food stores, Oriental markets, Chinese medicine shops, or online.

GREEN BAGS: A specially designed low-density polyethylene bag that dramatically extends the life of stored fresh fruits and vegetables. Ethylene gas is naturally released from fresh produce during storage and these handy reusable bags retard spoilage by absorbing and removing this damaging gas. Green bags come in a variety of sizes and can be purchased in natural foods stores or online.

GREEN SUPER FOODS: Different varieties of dried grass, grass juice, algae, kelp, and other healing foods dried and powdered into a green supplement. Spirulina, or blue-green algae, is an excellent source of chlorophyll, vitamins, minerals, and protein and has become a popular green smoothie addition over the years.

GRILL BASKET: A metal container used for grilling small pieces of food on the barbecue that might otherwise fall through the cracks.

HEMP SEED: A rich-and-nutty-flavored seed, high in protein, omega fatty acids, amino acids, and essential minerals. Hulled hemp seeds give smoothies a creamy texture and when ground, give breads a high quality protein boost.

JICAMA: A large beet-shaped root vegetable originally from Mexico. It has a thin brown skin and a crisp white flesh that tastes slightly sweet. Jicama can be eaten raw or cooked.

KAFFIR LIME LEAVES: An essential ingredient in Thai cuisine that infuses a distinctive lemon-lime flavor into soups and sauces. Fresh or frozen kaffir lime leaves can be purchased in Oriental grocery stores and stored in the freezer for up to one year.

KOMBU: See sea vegetables

LEMON GRASS: A long, thin grass-like herb used in Asian cuisine with a distinct sour lemon flavor. Purchase fresh stalks of lemon grass at the farmers market or in the produce section of natural foods stores. You can also find whole stalks and ground lemongrass in jars in the freezer section of most Asian markets.

MACA ROOT POWDER: An indigenous medicinal herb that comes from high in the Andes of Peru and is often used as a supplement in smoothies. Maca is high in calcium, magnesium, phosphorous, and iron, and also contains many essential trace minerals.

MANCHEGO CHEESE: A flavorful Spanish sheep's milk cheese that ranges from mild to sharp, depending on how long it has been aged. This semi-firm cheese is used in a wide variety of savory dishes, adding a distinctive nutty flavor.

MANDOLIN: A handy kitchen tool that quickly and uniformly slices firm vegetables and fruits. The blade can be adjusted to different thicknesses and designs, and will julienne and crinkle cut as well.

MASA HARINA: A finely ground corn flour traditionally used for making tamales and tortillas that has traces of lime for added calcium that helps to better assimilate the nutrients.

MILLET: A grain used by many cultures throughout the world and an excellent source of protein, B vitamins, and other essential nutrients. Millet is a good choice for those who are sensitive to gluten and can be made into a wide variety of dishes as a substitute for rice or other grains.

MIRIN: A sweet cooking wine made from rice and used in Japanese cooking. It adds a distinctive flavor to soups, sauces, and other savory dishes, and the alcohol content is usually less than one percent.

MISO: A fermented paste that can be made from soybeans, rice, barley, or buckwheat in a variety of styles. Miso is naturally salty and the flavors vary considerably—typically, the darker the

color of the miso, the saltier it is. This highly nutritious flavor enhancer and soup base provides healthy enzymes, beneficial microorganisms, and trace minerals.

MUSHROOM POWDER: A seasoning made from grinding dried mushrooms with a small food mill or coffee grinder. The easiest way to make mushroom powder is to use sliced and dried shiitake, porcini, or other varieties of mushrooms which can be found in the Oriental section of most grocery stores.

NAMA SHOYU: A raw or unpasteurized aged soy sauce made from organic soybeans with the healthy live enzymes still intact—unlike tamari and regular soy sauce.

NON-DAIRY MILK: Soy, rice, nut, and seed milks are found in nearly all supermarkets, or they can be freshly made at home, and used as a substitute for cow or goat milk with good results, depending on what you're making.

NORI: See sea vegetables.

NUTRITIONAL YEAST: This inactive yeast is rich in minerals and vitamins; and lends a nutty flavor to sauces, dressings, soups, and vegetable dishes. Nutritional yeast is a tasty low-fat and -sodium condiment that is a good source of protein and B vitamins. The flavors can vary considerably. Nutritional, or Brewers', yeast can be found in most natural food stores or online.

PAPADAM: A thin Indian cracker usually made from lentils and often flavored with garlic, chile, and cumin.

QUINOA: An ancient grain of the Incas that has been a staple of health conscious eaters since it migrated up from South America in the 60s. Quinoa has the highest protein content of any grain and is an excellent source of B vitamins, iron, calcium, potassium and vitamin E. It is a light and flavorful grain with a slightly crunchy texture and takes only 10–15 minutes to cook. Wash quinoa well before cooking and drain using a fine wire mesh strainer to remove the sapoins, the natural protective coating that can give it a bitter flavor. Quinoa is best when soaked for several hours, or overnight, rinsed well, and drained before cooking.

RICE PAPER WRAPPERS: Paper-thin sheets of rice used to make Thai or Vietnamese

spring or salad rolls. Most wrappers have a basket-like-weave design stamped into their round shape. They need to be softened in water before using and can take a little practice to master. Some wrappers have a tendency to fall apart easily and are more difficult to work with than others. I recommend using the Red Rose brand.

SEA VEGETABLES: Seaweed, or sea vegetables, are important foods commonly found in Japanese, macrobiotic, and raw cuisine. A good source of valuable nutrients and trace minerals, sea vegetables can be used to flavor soups, sauces, salads, crackers, and savory dishes. Kombu, wakame, hijiki, arame, and sea palm are the most common varieties. Nori sheets, used in making sushi rolls, are made from shredded and dried seaweed. There are many different varieties of seaweed and numerous drying techniques, and the best selections of quality sea vegetables can be found in Oriental markets, natural foods stores, or online.

SEITAN: Sometimes called wheat meat, this is a gluten protein product that can be substituted for chicken, seafood, or meat in many of your favorite dishes with nice results. Seitan is a good choice for those who are sensitive to soy but can tolerate wheat, both of which are often used in vegan versions of classic meat products. This versatile food can found in the refrigerator section of most natural food stores, online, or can also be made by hand. Seitan has a firm texture and seasoned slabs, or steaks lightly cooked on the grill and slathered with your favorite sauce, pesto, or fresh salsa is a great vegetarian offering for a barbecue.

SHIITAKE: A rich, woodsy mushroom with an umbrella-shaped brown cap often used in Chinese and Japanese cuisine. These flavorful mushrooms have numerous medicinal uses, including excellent support for the immune system. Look for them at farmers markets or in the produce sections of natural foods stores.

SLOW FOODS: A non-profit eco-organization founded to counteract the fast food and lifestyle that exists in much of the world today. The information they provide encourages us to question the food we eat, where it comes from, and how our choices affect the rest of the world. For more information, see www. slowfood.com.

SOLAR COOKERS: There are many different models of these resource-saving devices, from box ovens to curved panels and other unique designs. They require no fuel and use the energy of the sun to cook food and sterilize drinking water. For more information, see www. solarcooking.org.

SPELT: An ancient form of wheat that is easier to digest than the hybrid varieties we commonly use today. Spelt is a good choice for those with sensitivities or allergies and can be used in place of wheat flour with good results in most recipes.

SPIKE: An all-purpose seasoning made from salt, dehydrated land and sea vegetables, herbs, and spices that can be added to almost any savory dish for a little flavor boost. It can be purchased in any health food store, most supermarkets, or online.

SPROUTING BAGS: Gallon-size cotton, linen, nylon, or plastic mesh bags with a drawstring closure. Soaked seeds, nuts, and beans are hung in these handy bags for the allotted sprouting time. They are also used for straining blended nut milks and vegetable juices from their pulp.

SRIACHA: A popular Thai hot sauce made from hot red chiles, garlic, and salt that has a good balance of hot and sweet. A very tasty condiment, Sriacha can be found in most Oriental markets, but look for the brands made without preservatives.

STEVIA: An herbal extract made from the leaves of the stevia plant that is 250 to 300 times sweeter than white sugar, and has little effect on blood sugar levels in the body. Stevia is a naturally sweet herb that can be incorporated into any infusion for a non-caloric alternative sweetener.

SUCANAT: A natural sugar made from dehydrated cane juice that still contains the vitamins and minerals needed for proper digestion. Rapadura is also another type of evaporated cane juice that has not been refined. Both sucanat and rapadura can replace white sugar in most recipes.

TAHINI: Smooth high-protein butter made from sesame seeds with a texture a bit thicker than peanut butter.

Tahini has a rich nutty flavor and is an important ingredient in Middle Eastern cuisine. Raw or toasted tahini can be found in natural food stores or specialty sections of most markets.

TAMARI: A naturally brewed soy sauce that has a rich aroma and smooth full flavor. The taste of tamari is more balanced and less salty than regular soy sauce.

TAMARIND: The tart and acidic pulp from the fruit of the tamarind tree that is sold with pods or as a paste or concentrate, and is often used in Asian and Latin American cuisine.

TAPIOCA POWDER: To make, grind whole tapioca in a small coffee/herb grinder until it becomes a powder. Use as a clear thickener when making fresh fruit pies, tarts, and crisps.

TEMPEH: A cultured soy food, often flavored with the addition of grains, vegetables, and seaweed that has been a staple of Indonesia for generations. An excellent source of plant-based protein, containing all the essential amino acids and high in the vitamin B12, tempeh can be substituted for meat in many of your favorite dishes with a few simple techniques and a creative touch.

TOFU: A high-protein, soft, cheese-like bean curd made from cooked soybeans that is then filtered, pressed into blocks, and packaged in water. Tofu has little flavor of its own and absorbs whatever herbs, spices, or marinade you choose to season it with.

UNSALTED BUTTER: Unsalted, or sweet butter, preferably organic, is usually made from higher quality cream than the salted variety and is always the best choice for baking and making desserts.

VEGAN MAYONNAISE: An eggless and dairy-free mayonnaise alternative. Vegenaise brand is the freshest and most flavorful one I have found on the market and it can be found in the refrigerated section of most natural food stores.

VEGETABLE BROTH POWDER: A seasoning made from dehydrated vegetables, herbs, spices, and salt. It can be useful in flavoring soups, sauces, and other savory dishes as a substitute for freshly made stock. I recommend using organic brands, especially since the ingredients are concentrated.

VITA-MIX: This powerful machine does the work of several kitchen appliances. It blends, grinds, and prepares foods with ease and is the ultimate kitchen appliance for both home and professional use. If you can only afford to purchase one appliance, this is the one.

VITAL WHEAT GLUTEN: A powdered extract of whole wheat that helps to lighten the texture of whole grain breads.

WASABI: A Japanese horseradish powder that when blended with water forms a green paste. The paste is then mixed with soy sauce, tamari, or nama shoyu for a sushi dipping sauce.

WESTON PRICE FOUNDATION: A non-profit organization based on the work of Weston Price and committed to education, research, and activism as they relate to food, farming, and the healing arts. This is one of the best resources for current information on nutrition and other interesting food and health related topics. For more information, visit their website at www. westonaprice.org

YERBA MATÉ: A traditional South American green tea that has been a staple of indigenous diets for many generations. It is a mild stimulant, but lacks many of the negative effects of black tea or coffee and is best steeped in very hot, but not boiling water, to avoid a bitter taste.

YOGURT STARTER: A small amount of live cultured yogurt that when mixed with warm milk and allowed to sit at room temperature, becomes fresh yogurt. Starters can come from a store-bought plain yogurt that has living enzymes, or online from a number of sources.

Index

A

Agua Fresca, 20
Almond Wasabi Sauce, 103
Almonds, Breakfast Quinoa with Fresh
   Strawberries Blueberries, and, 37
Amphora Chocolate Cake, 176
Amphora Eggs Benedict, 46
Apple-Raspberry Crisp, 178
Artichokes, Granny's Stuffed, 111
Asian Cabbage Salad, 77
Asian Salad Rolls with Chile-Lime
   Dipping Sauce and Gado-Gado, 85
Avocado, and Slaw Salad
   Wrap, Hummus, 84

B

Baked Fish Fillet with Fresh
   Herb Crust, 119
Bali Toast, 39
Balsamic and Fresh Basil
   Vinaigrette, 92
Bars, Date Nut, 182
Basic Lemon and Olive
   Oil Dressing, 90
Basic Sweet Pie Dough, 169
Basic Vegetable Soup, 52
Beans,
      Black Bean Burritos, 106
      Chipotle Black Beans, 106
      Lima Bean, Shiitake, and
         Winter Vegetable Stew, 112
      Sprouting Seeds, Nuts,
      or Beans, 66–67
Beef and Mushroom Stroganoff,
   Grass-Fed, 127
Berry Smoothie, Kiwi, 22
Beverages, see also Smoothies
   and Vegetable Juices
      Agua Fresca, 20
      Carrot Cooler, 26
      Cherry, Peach, and Hemp
         Seed Smoothie, 23
      Citrus Cooler, 20
      Creamy Mango-Coconut
         Smoothie, 22
      Dreamy Cashew Date
         Smoothie, 24
      Fennel Combo, 26
      Green Goodness, 26
      Green Tea Chai, 29
      Hazelnut Hemp Mylk, 28
      Hot Carob Cocoa, 29

      Kiwi Berry Smoothie, 22
      Maté Latte, 30
      Pear and Feijoa Smoothie, 24
      Spicy Combo, 28
      Spinach Cooler, 27
      Tropical Delight Smoothie, 23
      V-6, 27
Big Batch Pizza, 109
Black Bean Burritos, 106
Black Beans, Chipotle, 106
Bliss Balls, 184
Blonde Baked Tart Shell, 173
Blueberries, and Almonds, Breakfast
   Quinoa with Fresh Strawberries, 37
Blueberry Pancakes, Multigrain, 40
Breads,
      Corn Tortillas, 154
      Grill Bread, 163
      Honey Whole Grain Bread, 164
      Sourdough English Muffins, 162
      Sourdough Rye Bread, 161
      Traditional Whole Grain
         Sourdough Bread, 158
      Whole Grain Scones, 166
      Whole Grain Tortillas
      or Chapatis, 155
Breakfast Quinoa with Fresh
   Strawberries, Blueberries,
   and Almonds, 37
Breakfast, Samurai, 48
Broccolini, Mushroom, and
   Provolone Strata, 113
Brown Rice Cream with Dates,
   Cinnamon, and Vanilla, 36
Buckwheat Pancakes, Sourdough, 41
Burritos, Black Bean, 106
Butternut Squash Pie with
   Maple Whipped Cream, 170

C

Cabbage and Pineapple
   Salad, Red, 78
Cabbage Salad, Asian, 77
Cake, Amphora Chocolate, 176
Calzone, 109
Candy, Yam, 183
Carob Cocoa, Hot, 29
Carrot Cooler, 26
Cashew Date Smoothie, Dreamy, 24
Cashew Pesto, Fusion Lentil
   Soup with Basil and, 56
Chai, Green Tea, 29
Chanterelle Gravy, 63
Chapatis, Whole Grain Tortillas or, 155
Chard Enchiladas, Tempeh and, 100
Chard Pie, 105

Cheese,
      Ricotta Cheesecake, 175
      Simple Fresh Cheese, 143
      Yogurt Cheese, 142
Cheesecake, Ricotta, 175
Cherry Pecan Tart, Fresh, 174
Cherry, Peach, and Hemp
   Seed Smoothie, 23
Chicken,
      Chicken Dijon with Fresh Dill, 122
      Chicken Soup, Indonesian, 55
      Garden Herb and Lemon
         Chicken, 121
Chile Sauce, Red, 59
Chile-Lime Dipping Sauce and
   Gado-Gado, Asian Salad
   Rolls with, 85
Chile-Lime Dressing, South-of-
   the-Border Slaw with, 76
Chipotle Black Beans, 106
Chipotle Thousand Island, 95
Chocolate,
      Amphora Chocolate Cake, 176
      Chocolate Ganache, 174
      Luscious Chocolate Frosting, 177
Chunky Guacamole Salad, 80
Citrus Cooler, 20
Cocoa, Hot Carob, 29
Coconut Smoothie,
      Creamy Mango-, 22
Company Kitchari, 101
Cookies, Golden Oatmeal, 181
Corn Tortillas, 154
Crackers, Handmade Whole Grain 156
Cranberry-Tangerine Relish, 138
Creamy Cilantro Dressing, 96
Creamy Mango-Coconut Smoothie, 22
Creamy Sesame Sauce, 103
Crème Fraîche, 144
Crisp, Apple-Raspberry, 178
Crispy Tempeh Crumbles, 146
Croutons, Whole Grain, 148
Cucumber, Yogurt, and Mint Salad, 79

D

Dates,
      Brown Rice Cream with Dates,
         Cinnamon, and Vanilla, 36
      Date Nut Bars, 182
      Dreamy Cashew Date
         Smoothie, 24
Dreamy Cashew Date Smoothie, 24
Dreamy Tahini, 93
Dressings, Salad,
      Balsamic and Fresh Basil
         Vinaigrette, 92

Basic Lemon and Olive
  Oil Dressing, 90
Chipotle Thousand Island, 95
Creamy Cilantro Dressing, 96
Fresh Herb Vinaigrette, 91
Green Goddess, 95
Kale and Sea Vegetable Salad
  with Sesame Citrus Dressing, 87
Kiwi Vinaigrette, 92
Rockin' Ranch, 94
Roquefort Vinaigrette, 90
South-of-the-Border Slaw with
  Chile-Lime Dressing, 76
White Miso, Grapefruit,
  and Flax seed oil, 94
Dried Fruit Compote, 38

E
Edible Flowers, 73
Eggs Benedict, Amphora, 46
Enchiladas, Tempeh and Chard, 100
English Muffins, Sourdough, 162

F
Feijoa Smoothie, Pear and, 24
Fennel Combo, 26
Fennel, and Tangerine Salad with
  Maple Pecans, Spinach, 81
Fish,
        Baked Fish Fillet with Fresh
          Herb Crust, 119
        Grilled Whole Fish, 117
        Grilled Wild Salmon Fillet with
          Thai Cilantro Pesto, 118
Flowers, Edible, 73
Focaccia, 110
Fresh,
        Fresh Cherry Pecan Tart, 174
        Fresh Herb Vinaigrette, 91
        Fresh Mint and Raisin Sauce, 62
        Fresh Summer Fruit Tart with
          Honey Citrus Cream, 172
        Fresh Vegetable Platter with
          Assorted Dips, 131
        Fresh Vegetable Stock, 51
        Grilled Leg of Lamb with Fresh
          Mint and Raisin Sauce, 128
        Quick Fresh Raspberry Jam, 177
Frosting, Luscious Chocolate, 177
Fruits,
        Apple-Raspberry Crisp, 178
        Basic Lemon and Olive
          Oil Dressing, 90
        Breakfast Quinoa with Fresh
          Strawberries Blueberries,
          and Almonds, 37

Brown Rice Cream with Dates,
  Cinnamon, and Vanilla, 36
Cherry, Peach, and Hemp
  Seed Smoothie, 23
Citrus Cooler, 20
Cranberry-Tangerine Relish, 138
Creamy Mango-Coconut
  Smoothie, 22
Dreamy Cashew Date
  Smoothie, 24
Dried Fruit Compote, 38
Fresh Cherry Pecan Tart, 174
Fresh Mint and Raisin Sauce, 62
Fresh Summer Fruit Tart with
  Honey Citrus Cream, 172
Garden Herb and Lemon
  Chicken, 121
Kiwi Berry Smoothie, 22
Kiwi Vinaigrette, 92
Live Oat and Tropical
  Fruit Muesli, 34
Multigrain Blueberry Pancakes, 40
Pear and Feijoa Smoothie, 24
Pineapple Teriyaki Sauce, 61
Quick Fresh Raspberry Jam, 177
Red Cabbage and
  Pineapple Salad, 78
Spicy Pear Pie, 171
Spinach, Fennel, and Tangerine
  Salad with Maple Pecans, 81
White Miso, Grapefruit, and
  Flax seed oil Dressing, 94
Fusion Lentil Soup with Basil
  and Cashew Pesto, 56

G
Gado-Gado, 62
Gado-Gado, Asian Salad Rolls with
  Chile-Lime Dipping Sauce and, 85
Gado-Gado, Indonesian
  Tempeh Sticks with, 98
Ganache, Chocolate, 174
Garden Herb and Lemon Chicken, 121
Garden Pesto, 136
Ghee, 150
Golden Oatmeal Cookies, 181
Gomasio, 149
Grains,
        Golden Oatmeal Cookies, 181
        Handmade Whole Grain
          Crackers, 156
        Honey Whole Grain Bread, 164
        Multigrain Blueberry Pancakes, 40
        Multigrain Pizza, 108
        Rice Cream with Dates, Cinnamon,
          and Vanilla, Brown, 36

Quinoa with Fresh Strawberries,
  Blueberries, and Almonds,
  Breakfast, 37
Sourdough Buckwheat
  Pancakes, 41
Sourdough Rye Bread, 161
Traditional Whole Grain
  Sourdough Bread, 158
Whole Grain Croutons, 148
Whole Grain Scones, 166
Whole Grain Tortillas
  or Chapatis, 155
Granny's Stuffed Artichokes, 111
Granola, Living Rise and Shine, 32
Grapefruit, and Flax seed oil
  Dressing, White Miso, 94
Grass-Fed Beef and Mushroom
  Stroganoff, 127
Gravy, Chanterelle, 63
Gravy, Tahini-Miso, 64
Green Goddess, Dressing, 95
Green Goodness, 26
Green Tea Chai, 29
Grill Bread, 163
Grilled Leg of Lamb with Fresh
  Mint and Raisin Sauce, 128
Grilled Whole Fish, 117
Grilled Wild Salmon Fillet with
  Thai Cilantro Pesto, 118
Guacamole Salad, Chunky, 80

H
Handmade Whole Grain Crackers, 156
Hazelnut Hemp Mylk, 28
Hemp Mylk, Hazelnut, 28
Hemp Seed Smoothie,
  Cherry, Peach and, 23
Homemade Yogurt, 141
Honey Citrus Cream, Fresh
  Summer Fruit Tart with, 172
Honey Whole Grain Bread, 164
Hot Carob Cocoa, 29
Huevos Rancheros, 45
Hummus, 132
Hummus, Avocado, and
  Slaw Salad Wrap, 84

I
Indonesian Chicken Soup, 55
Indonesian Tempeh Sticks
  with Gado-Gado, 98

J
Jam, Quick Fresh Raspberry, 177
Jewel Salad, 88

K

Kale and Sea Vegetable Salad with
  Sesame Citrus Dressing, 87
Kitchari, Company, 101
Kiwi Berry Smoothie, 22
Kiwi Vinaigrette, 92

L

Lamb with Fresh Mint and Raisin
  Sauce, Grilled Leg of, 128
Latte, Maté, 30
Lemon and Olive Oil
  Dressing, Basic, 90
Lemon Chicken, Garden Herb and, 121
Lentil Soup with Basil and
  Cashew Pesto, Fusion, 56
Lettuces and Greens, see page 69-70
Lima Bean, Shiitake, and Winter
  Vegetable Stew, 112
Live Oat and Tropical Fruit Muesli, 34
Living Rise and Shine Granola, 32
Luscious Chocolate Frosting, 177

M

Mango-Coconut Smoothie, Creamy 22
Maple Whipped Cream, Butternut
  Squash Pie with, 170
Maté Latte, 30
Mayonnaise from Scratch, 139
Miso,
    Miso Vegetable Soup, 54
    Tahini-Miso Gravy, 64
    White Miso, Grapefruit, and
      Flax seed oil Dressing, 94
Muesli, Live Oat and Tropical Fruit, 34
Multigrain Blueberry Pancakes, 40
Multigrain Pizza, 108
Mushrooms,
    Broccolini, Mushroom, and
      Provolone Strata, 113
    Chanterelle Gravy, 63
    Grass-Fed Beef and Mushroom
      Stroganoff, 127
    Lima Bean, Shiitake, and
      Winter Vegetable Stew, 112

N

Nuts,
    Almond Wasabi Sauce, 103
    Breakfast Quinoa with Fresh
      Strawberries, Blueberries,
      and Almonds, 37
    Date Nut Bars, 182
    Dreamy Cashew Date
      Smoothie, 24

Fresh Cherry Pecan Tart, 174
Fusion Lentil Soup with Basil
  and Cashew Pesto, 56
Hazelnut Hemp Mylk, 28
Sprouting Seeds, Nuts,
  or Beans, 66–67
Spinach, Fennel, and Tangerine
  Salad with Maple Pecans, 81
Tamari-Toasted Nuts
  and Seeds, 147
Nut Milks; see Hazelnut
  Hemp Mylk, 28

O

Oat and Tropical Fruit Muesli, Live, 34
Oatmeal Cookies, Golden, 181
Oatmeal, Perfect, 35
Olive and Sun-Dried Tomato
  Tapenade, 134

P

Pancakes, Multigrain Blueberry, 40
Pancakes, Sourdough Buckwheat, 41
Pasta with Tempeh Crumbles,
  Pescadero Pesto, 99
Peach, and Hemp Seed
  Smoothie, Cherry, 23
Pear and Feijoa Smoothie, 24
Pear Pie, Spicy, 171
Pecan Tart, Fresh Cherry, 174
Pecans, Spinach, Fennel, and
  Tangerine Salad with Maple, 81
Perfect Oatmeal, 35
Pescadero Pesto Pasta with
  Tempeh Crumbles, 99
Pesto,
    Fusion Lentil Soup with Basil
      and Cashew Pesto, 56
    Garden Pesto, 136
    Grilled Wild Salmon Fillet with
      Thai Cilantro Pesto, 118
    Pescadero Pesto Pasta with
      Tempeh Crumbles, 99
    Thai Cilantro Pesto, 137
Pie Dough, Basic Sweet, 169
Pies,
    Butternut Squash Pie with
      Maple Whipped Cream, 170
    Chard Pie, 105
    Spicy Pear Pie, 171
Pineapple Salad, Red
  Cabbage and, 78
Pineapple Teriyaki Sauce, 61
Pizza, Big Batch, 109
Pizza, Multigrain 108
Ponzu Sauce, 152

Poultry,
    Chicken Dijon with Fresh Dill, 122
    Garden Herb and Lemon
      Chicken, 121
    Smoked Turkey with Maple-
      Herb Brine, 124
    Turkey Loaf, 123
Provolone Strata, Broccolini,
  Mushroom, and, 113

Q

Quick Fresh Raspberry Jam, 177

R

Raisin Sauce, Fresh Mint and, 62
Raspberry Crisp, Apple-, 178
Raspberry Jam, Quick Fresh, 177
Red Cabbage and Pineapple Salad, 78
Red Chile Sauce, 59
Relish, Cranberry-Tangerine, 138
Rice Cream with Dates, Cinnamon,
  and Vanilla, Brown, 36
Ricotta Cheesecake, 175
Roasted Tomatillo Sauce, 60
Rockin' Ranch Dressing, 94
Romesco Sauce, 133
Roquefort Vinaigrette, 90

S

Salads,
    Asian Cabbage Salad, 77
    Asian Salad Rolls with
      Chile-Lime Dipping Sauce
      and Gado-Gado, 85
    Chunky Guacamole Salad, 80
    Cucumber, Yogurt, and
      Mint Salad, 79
    Hummus, Avocado, and
      Slaw Salad Wrap, 84
    Jewel Salad, 88
    Kale and Sea Vegetable Salad
      with Sesame Citrus Dressing, 87
    Red Cabbage and
      Pineapple Salad, 78
    Simple Fall Slaw, 75
    South-of-the-Border Slaw with
      Chile-Lime Dressing, 76
    Spinach, Fennel, and Tangerine
      Salad with Maple Pecans, 81
    Tempeh Salad, 82
Salmon Fillet with Thai Cilantro
  Pesto, Grilled Wild, 118
Salsa Fresca, 135
Samurai Breakfast, 48
Sauces,
    Almond Wasabi Sauce, 103

Asian Salad Rolls with
    Chile-Lime Dipping Sauce
    and Gado-Gado, 85
Creamy Sesame Sauce, 103
Fresh Mint and Raisin Sauce, 62
Gado-Gado, 62
Pineapple Teriyaki Sauce, 61
Ponzu Sauce, 152
Red Chile Sauce, 59
Roasted Tomatillo Sauce, 60
Romesco Sauce, 133
Sun-Dried Tomato Sauce, 58
Traditional Wasabi Sauce, 102
Scones, Whole Grain, 166
Scrambled Tofu and Fresh Veggies, 42
Sea Vegetable Salad with Sesame
    Citrus Dressing, Kale and, 87
Seeds,
    Cherry, Peach, and
        Hemp Seed, 23
    Creamy Sesame Sauce, 103
    Sprouting Seeds, Nuts,
        or Beans, 66–67
    Tamari-Toasted Nuts
        and Seeds, 147
Sesame Sauce, Creamy, 103
Shiitake, and Winter Vegetable
    Stew, Lima Bean, 112
Simple Fall Slaw, 75
Simple Fresh Cheese, 143
Slaws,
    Hummus, Avocado, and
        Slaw Salad Wrap, 84
    Simple Fall Slaw, 75
    South-of-the-Border Slaw with
        Chile-Lime Dressing, 76
Smoked Turkey with Maple-
    Herb Brine, 124
Smoothies
    Cherry, Peach, and
        Hemp Seed, 23
    Creamy Mango-Coconut, 22
    Dreamy Cashew Date, 24
    Kiwi Berry, 22
    Pear and Feijoa, 24
    Tropical Delight, 23
Soups and Stews,
    Basic Vegetable Soup, 52
    Fresh Vegetable Stock, 51
    Fusion Lentil Soup with Basil
        and Cashew Pesto, 56
    Indonesian Chicken Soup, 55
    Lima Bean, Shiitake, and
        Winter Vegetable Stew, 112
    Miso Vegetable Soup, 54
    Sunshine Yam Soup, 57

Sourdough,
    Sourdough Buckwheat
        Pancakes, 41
    Sourdough English Muffins, 162
    Sourdough Rye Bread, 161
    Sourdough Starter, 157
    Traditional Whole Grain
        Sourdough Bread, 158
South-of-the-Border Slaw with
    Chile-Lime Dressing, 76
Spicy Combo, 28
Spicy Pear Pie, 171
Spinach Cooler, 27
Spinach, Fennel, and Tangerine
    Salad with Maple Pecans, 81
Sprouting Seeds, Nuts,
    or Beans, 66–67
Stock, Fresh Vegetable, 51
Strata, Broccolini, Mushroom,
    and Provolone, 113
Strawberries, Blueberries,
    and Almonds, Breakfast
    Quinoa with Fresh, 37
Stroganoff, Grass-Fed Beef
    and Mushroom, 127
Sun-Dried Tomato Sauce, 58
Sun-Dried Tomato Tapenade,
    Olive and, 134
Sunshine Yam Soup, 57
Sushi Rolls with Three
    Sauces, Veggie, 102

T
Tahini, Dreamy, 93
Tahini-Miso Gravy, 64
Tamari-Toasted Nuts and Seeds, 147
Tangerine Relish, Cranberry-, 138
Tangerine Salad with Maple Pecans,
    Spinach, Fennel, and, 81
Tapenade, Olive and Sun-
    Dried Tomato, 134
Tarts,
    Blonde Baked Tart Shell, 173
    Fresh Cherry Pecan Tart, 174
    Fresh Summer Fruit Tart with
        Honey Citrus Cream, 172
    Tart Shell, 172
Tea Chai, Green, 29
Tempeh,
    Crispy Tempeh Crumbles, 146
    Indonesian Tempeh Sticks
        with Gado-Gado, 98
    Pescadero Pesto Pasta with
        Tempeh Crumbles, 99
    Tempeh and Chard
        Enchiladas, 100

Tempeh Salad, 82
Teriyaki Sauce, Pineapple, 61
Thai Cilantro Pesto, 137
Thai Cilantro Pesto, Grilled Wild
    Salmon Fillet with, 118
Toast, Bali, 39
Tofu and Fresh Veggies,
    Scrambled, 42
Tomatillo Sauce, Roasted, 60
Tomato Sauce, Sun-Dried, 58
Tortillas, Corn, 154
Tortillas or Chapatis,
    Whole Grain, 155
Traditional Wasabi Sauce, 102
Traditional Whole Grain
    Sourdough Bread, 158
Tropical Delight Smoothie, 23
Tropical Fruit Muesli, Live Oat and, 34
Turkey Loaf, 123
Turkey with Maple-Herb
    Brine, Smoked, 124

V
V-6, 27
Vegetables,
    Asian Cabbage Salad, 77
    Basic Vegetable Soup, 52
    Broccolini, Mushroom, and
        Provolone Strata, 113
    Butternut Squash Pie with
        Maple Whipped Cream, 170
    Chard Pie, 105
    Chunky Guacamole Salad, 80
    Cucumber, Yogurt, and
        Mint Salad, 79
    Fresh Vegetable Platter with
        Assorted Dips, 131
    Fresh Vegetable Stock, 51
    Granny's Stuffed Artichokes, 111
    Hummus, Avocado, and
        Slaw Salad Wrap, 84
    Kale and Sea Vegetable Salad
        with Sesame Citrus Dressing, 87
    Lettuces and Greens,
        see page 69-70
    Lima Bean, Shiitake, and
        Winter Vegetable Stew, 112
    Miso Vegetable Soup, 54
    Olive and Sun-Dried Tomato
        Tapenade, 134
    Red Cabbage and
        Pineapple Salad, 78
    Roasted Tomatillo Sauce, 60
    Scrambled Tofu and
        Fresh Veggies, 42
    Simple Fall Slaw, 75

South-of-the-Border Slaw with
Chile-Lime Dressing, 76
Spinach, Fennel, and Tangerine
Salad with Maple Pecans, 81
Sun-Dried Tomato Sauce, 58
Sunshine Yam Soup, 57
Tempeh and Chard
Enchiladas, 100
Vegetable Juices
Carrot Cooler, 26
Fennel Combo, 26
Green Goodness, 26
Spicy Combo, 28
Spinach Cooler, 27
V-6, 27
Veggie Loaf, 114
Veggie Sushi Rolls with
Three Sauces, 102
Yam Candy, 183
Veggie Loaf, 114
Veggie Sushi Rolls with
Three Sauces, 102
Veggies, Scrambled Tofu
and Fresh, 42

Vinaigrettes,
Balsamic and Fresh Basil
Vinaigrette, 92
Fresh Herb Vinaigrette, 91
Kiwi Vinaigrette, 92
Roquefort Vinaigrette, 90

W
Wasabi Sauce, Almond, 103
Wasabi Sauce, Traditional, 102
White Miso, Grapefruit, and
Flax seed oil Dressing, 94
Whole Grain,
Handmade Whole Grain
Crackers, 156
Honey Whole Grain Bread, 164
Traditional Whole Grain
Sourdough Bread, 158
Whole Grain Croutons, 148
Whole Grain Scones, 166
Whole Grain Tortillas
or Chapatis, 155
Winter Vegetable Stew, Lima
Bean, Shiitake, and, 112

Y
Yam Candy, 183
Yam Soup, Sunshine 57
Yogurt,
Yogurt, and Mint Salad,
Cucumber, 79
Yogurt Cheese, 142
Yogurt, Homemade, 141

Metric Conversion Chart

Volume Measurements		Weight Measurements		Temperature Conversion	
U.S.	METRIC	U.S.	METRIC	FAHRENHEIT	CELSIUS
1 teaspoon	5 ml	1/2 ounce	15 g	250	120
1 tablespoon	15 ml	1 ounce	30 g	300	150
1/4 cup	60 ml	3 ounces	90 g	325	160
1/3 cup	75 ml	4 ounces	115 g	350	180
1/2 cup	125 ml	8 ounces	225 g	375	190
2/3 cup	150 ml	12 ounces	350 g	400	200
3/4 cup	175 ml	1 pound	450 g	425	220
1 cup	250 ml	2 1/4 pounds	1 kg	450	230